The Challenge of Human Diversity

The Challenge of Human Diversity

Mirrors, Bridges, and Chasms

DeWight R. Middleton

State University of New York College, Oswego

WAVELAND
PRESS, INC.
Prospect Heights, Illinois

For information about this book, write or call:
    Waveland Press, Inc.
    P.O. Box 400
    Prospect Heights, Illinois 60070
    (847) 634-0081

Contents

Acknowledgments   vii

Introduction: The Challenge of Diversity   **1**
Understanding Diversity   2
The Strategy of Anthropology   3
Plan of the Book   5

1 Culture Shock   **7**
Shocks to the System   8
  Challenges to the Senses   9
  Communicating   11
  Social Use of Food   14
  Gender Roles   17
  Moral Dilemmas   19
Intracultural Jolts   21
Conclusion   22

2 Common Ground   **23**
Brain, Mind, and Evolution   24
Social Race   26
Thought, Emotions, and Culture   28
  Perception and Cognition   28
  Emotions   33
  Culture   35
Channeling Behavior   39
  Socialization and Social Identity   39
  Role, Status, and Self   40
  Morality   41
Conclusion   42

3   Our Lived Difference   **45**

Culture as Adaptation   46
   Poverty: African-American Inner Cities, 1960s   48
   Poverty: Urban Italy   51
   Poverty: The Santa Clara Canning Industry   53
Culture as Meaning   56
   Meaning: Sensory Experience   57
   Intracultural Meanings   59
Culture as System   59
   Gender Roles   60
   Ethnicity   62
Conclusion   64

4   Mirrors and Chasms   **65**

Colonialism and Racism   66
   Decline and Degeneration   67
The Noble Savage   68
Indigenous Response and Resistance   69
Images and Myths   72
   The Power of Images   72
   The Educated Eye   74
   The Myth of Africa   77
Native Resurgence and Political Actions   80
Conclusion   82

5   Mirrors and Voices   **83**

Historical Background to Fieldwork   83
The Shock of the New   86
The Dialogue of Fieldwork   89
Observation and Participation   91
   Response Effects   92
   Rapport   93
   Objective Distance and Repositioning   94
Intracultural Diversities   96
Ethics   97
Conclusion   98

6   Meeting the Challenge   **99**

References   **103**
Index   **109**

Acknowledgments

This small book is the result of a larger collaborative effort, although I am alone responsible for whatever shortcomings it might have. I want to thank my friend and undergraduate mentor, David L. Scruton, for casting his ever critical eye on various versions of the manuscript, and my graduate school chum, Constance deRoche, for her detailed and insightful comments at a critical juncture of its preparation. Several reviewers offered useful suggestions as well. I want to acknowledge my colleague, Ivan Brady, for his general advice and support, but even more so for many years of productive discussions about curriculum and classroom. I owe much to my daughters, Leida and Chandra, and my wife, Peg, for suffering in good humor my periodic and extended disappearances into the den, and for their invaluable service in retyping an earlier draft to replace the one that mysteriously disappeared from my computer one day. Finally, my thanks to Tom Curtin and Jeni Ogilvie at Waveland for their friendly professionalism.

Introduction

The Challenge of Diversity

The police beat a black man in Los Angeles, provoking a national discussion of race and police brutality, and later sparking a riot in South Central Los Angeles. American public opinion rises against illegal Mexican and Haitian immigrants. Gays fight for equality in the American military. In Germany, skinheads terrorize foreign workers. The Soviet empire collapses and Yugoslavia disintegrates into ethnic hatred and killing as Croats, Serbs, and Muslims strike out against each other. Iraqis gas Kurds in northern Iraq, while Hutus and Tutsis slaughter each other in Burundi. The French-speaking Province of Quebec attempts to secede from Canada. Native peoples of the world's rain forests suffer ecological, cultural, and personal assaults from outsiders in the name of progress.

Problems arising from human diversity are widespread, persistent, and often intractable; they challenge severely our ability to cope with differences on intellectual and practical levels. In part, our problems in coping with issues of human diversity stem from simple misinformation, misunderstanding, and ignorant speculation about the meaning of physical and cultural differences. In part, they spring from a history of suspicion and cycles of violence and revenge between groups that sustain antagonistic relationships and impede rapprochement between them. Ignorance and troubled histories are churned by political and economic competition that further muddy our thinking about matters of diversity. Learning how to unravel the tangled complexities that often prevail in group relationships will take us a long way toward grasping the critical variables operating in specific cases of trouble.

Clearly, we cannot escape issues of diversity; they are all around us. Staying at home certainly will not insulate us; barely a handful of culturally homogeneous nations exist today (Nielsson 1985). If anything, comprehending diversity at home may be even more difficult because it is more immediate, threatening, and inescapable. Social dis-

1

tance need not be matched by great geographical distance to cause mischief. The fact is, however, that more people will continue to travel abroad as the tempo of international business transactions and tourism accelerates. College students are entering study abroad programs in increasing numbers. The world is increasingly interconnected electronically with voice, image, and text, raising international questions of standards, access, and control. Will these be new arenas for culture wars or for further cultural homogenization?

We are faced, then, with the pressing need to develop the art of living together by striking a balance between our differences and similarities. Cultural chasms develop out of our differences, real or imagined, but we can build bridges across these divides based on our similarities. We can do so, however, only if we are willing, by observing others, to look at ourselves in a cultural mirror and thereby see ourselves in a fresh light. This means that we all need to learn to understand others and ourselves and to identify the critical historical and competitive contexts in which we conduct our dialogue with each other.

UNDERSTANDING DIVERSITY

The problems of human diversity are complex, widespread, and continuing. The purpose of this book is to meet the challenge of human diversity by supplying the reader with the necessary information, concepts, and perspectives to grasp the dynamics of human interaction at both group and personal levels. At its conclusion, the reader will be better able to think analytically and critically about differences and similarities among human groups, to appreciate personally the risks and the rewards of engaging others, and to understand the necessity for making the effort in the first place.

Acquiring a framework of understanding and making a genuine effort to address issues will permit us to establish the solid base we need in order to understand how deep cultural differences are formed and maintained. Further, the lessons learned in this effort also can be applied to gender and class differences, and differences arising out of disease and handicap. They apply even to various units within complex organizations, for example, differences among college students, faculty, administration, and support staff. Wherever differences are generated and become impediments to establishing common ground, these lessons will apply. This is not just an agenda for a dominant majority to understand victimized minorities, but for all groups to understand each other and themselves.

This book is about human diversity, not multiculturalism. By human diversity, we mean both biological and physical variations and their significance in various natural and social environments around the world. In cultural anthropology, we do cross-cultural studies of two or more cultures for scientific reasons using established standards of comparison.

Multiculturalism, on the other hand, is a social and political movement advocating the good of having different cultures in the same society, especially in the United States (Eller 1997). It takes a moral tone and has to do with the "identity politics" of minorities against a perceived Eurocentric attitude, particularly in education. A group is validated by its culture. In this view, cultures are seen as different but equal (Eller 1997:252), a view that leads to a struggle against cultural dominance, or "culture wars." Eller concludes that anthropology should not be for or against multiculturalism, but stand ready to challenge erroneous claims on both sides and to foster a more sophisticated view of what is meant by cultural relativism from a critical perspective. This is precisely our purpose in this book.

THE STRATEGY OF ANTHROPOLOGY

The strategy used by cultural anthropology to comprehend other ways of life is simply stated: (1) *direct contact*, (2) *extended contact*, and (3) a *comparative perspective*. The principle of direct contact compels one to live with others on their own turf, generally under their conditions. No armchair philosophizing will do, nor imaginative discussions over cocktails, nor sharing of mutual ignorance, stereotypes, or preconceptions. Whether you are observing people in a jungle, a central city ghetto, or a middle-class suburb, you must go where they are and not speculate about them from afar.

Extended contact means that you can't just drop in for a day or two, give a questionnaire, and leave. It means you spend quality research time and participate in daily life as much as permitted. It means days, months, years of effort depending on the nature of the research and real-life contingencies. If necessary you must learn another language. Then you must attempt to place that particular experience and understanding in a larger, comparative context that enhances our general understanding of the human condition in both its universal and local expressions.

This book does not assume that the reader is or wants to be an anthropologist. It does advance the idea that the lessons anthropologists offer are time-tested and fire-hardened and that they can enhance the nonprofessional's grasp of human diversity. The methods are not perfect, and they yield imperfect results. Yet, they are based on those important principles that often work to improve human relationships even without anthropological expertise: a serious, extended and informed effort to tap into the experience of others and to see the world from their point of view. Doing so does not mean that you agree with their point of view, or behavior, but, of course, they have the same options about your presence. On the other hand, the result of enlightened effort, while not reaching a professional level, is more likely to be an informed and reflective engagement leading to better communication.

Anthropologists have discovered historically that the road to understanding other cultures is littered with hazards for which there are few warning signs to heed. The road has taken us much longer to travel and the destination of objective knowledge found to be more elusive than we first thought it would be. Nevertheless, the experiences of anthropologists speak eloquently of the road's difficulty of travel, and therefore will be instructive in building our framework. It is a road worth traveling.

Offered as the core of this book is the following argument: all humans are essentially the same and share the same basic capacity for thinking and feeling as well as for social and moral reasoning. This general capacity takes specific cultural shape as particular groups of humans endeavor to survive in different environments and historical situations. A critically important part of human efforts to fashion a living in the desert, or in the jungle, or in cities, adjacent to other humans, is to construct over time a cultural tradition, a continuing set of shared customs, knowledge, and beliefs that helps them to reach their goals . . . a blueprint for living.

Because each of us is emotionally and habitually committed to a tradition, we find it difficult to break its bounds. But we can, with earnest and informed effort, weaken our tradition's constraints sufficiently to come to know a different way of life. Individuals have done so for centuries. The secret in accomplishing this task lies in mapping the problems, interests, and experiences of people from their point of view, while striving to control the bias of our own tradition. Toward this end, we will build a framework of analysis that handles the fact that all cultures bear both similarities and differences and explains why it is often so hard for people to communicate across cultural borders (Brown 1991; Hall 1990).

Cultural anthropology is one of four principal divisions of anthropology. *Biological*, or *physical*, *anthropology* is devoted to the study of human evolution, primate behavior, human biological variation and adaptation, and human genetics. *Anthropological linguistics* analyzes language in its local expression and universal characteristics, explores its acquisition and development in children, and studies variations in linguistic performance in the same language as a result of differences in such variables as gender, geographical region, ethnicity, and social class. The latter subdiscipline is called *sociolinguistics*. The fourth division is *archaeology* which reconstructs ways of life from the physical remains of prehistoric cultures such as the ancient Maya in Central America. Archaeologists trace the transformations of a culture like the Maya from an early formative stage to its classic stage, and final collapse. In recent years, historical anthropology has become more popular as has underwater and urban archaeology. While we at times use the insights about human diversity gained from these fields, we will not otherwise address them here.

PLAN OF THE BOOK

We confront directly the challenge of visiting other cultures in chapter 1, "Culture Shock," where we explore the process of fitting into another culture and give particular attention to understanding what various cross-cultural incidents tell us about this uncertain process.

In chapter 2, "Our Common Ground," we define our commonality rather than our differences. We trace our origins, examine our senses, understand how we structure experience, and note some universal characteristics of human culture. Chapter 3, "Our Lived Difference," describes how we become different through our lived experience, how this experience of time and place contributes to what we do, what we believe, and what we value.

In chapter 4, "Mirrors and Chasms," we let others speak to us about their experiences in contact with us, and we re-examine as well our own progress in revealing our ethnocentrism (judging another culture by the standards of our own). We note the resurgence of minority groups around the world. In chapter 5, "Mirrors and Voices," we return to the central issue of establishing effective discourse with others through direct contact. Here we probe much deeper into the dynamics of dialogic exchanges, to the deeper levels of ethnocentricity that sometimes make productive communication so elusive. In the final chapter, "Meeting the Challenge," we summarize our argument and draw our conclusions.

Chapter One

Culture Shock

> The English were quite right. One had to dress for dinner. One needed a symbol, some external sign, to assist daily remembrance of what one was. It did not occur to me that the need for such artificial aids was alien to me and a sign that I was no longer myself. Instead, to help me over the next seven weeks, I called the cook and gave detailed orders for a Thanksgiving dinner. At the same time I told Sunday to lay out evening clothes, set the table with my best, and put out all the liquor in a fine array. I was no longer trying to learn how to survive in my new environment; I was concerned with sealing myself off from it. (Bowen [1954] 1964:238–39)

When we visit another country we customarily complain about a variety of problems. We find the place too hot, too cold, too wet, or too dry. We encounter foods that sicken us, odors that nauseate us, and sights that startle us. We worry about standards of sanitation and chafe at the lack of bathroom facilities. The "locals" act in strange ways for reasons we cannot fathom. Small children mill about us speaking with ease a language that eludes our adult comprehension. We are treated as curiosities. An alien way of life challenges our most cherished beliefs about who we are, who they are, and the nature of the world we both live in.

Burdened by these new challenges to our familiar way of life we might respond in anger, depression, or paranoia. Longing for the familiar, we might seek others like ourselves, and search for accustomed food. Withdrawing to the security of our rooms, we might lose ourselves in escapist novels and daydreams of the home we know so well. We might, as Bowen notes about her efforts to adjust to fieldwork in Africa, attempt to seal ourselves off for a time from the alien culture.

These responses are symptoms of culture shock. *Culture shock is defined as individual maladaptive behavior emerging under the stress of coping with a foreign way of life*. It is quite natural to feel fatigue and confusion and to seek periods of rest when living in another culture, but when occasional struggle advances to more persistent feelings of hostility and irritability, culture shock has seized us. We become frustrated because we cannot figure out what is going on, or why. These are the rough bumps that threaten to throw us off the road to personal adjustment to a new culture. Culture shock is a painful personal revelation of the profound extent to which we are emotionally and intellectually bound by our experience of growing up in a particular culture. It is also a striking reminder of how exceedingly difficult it can be for us to change our habitual way of life. It is a dramatic example of a human paradox that on the one hand our success as a species is utterly dependent on our ability to find novel solutions to vexing problems, while, on the other hand, it is novelty that we so often seek to avoid. This curious blend of commitment to both tradition and change, as individuals or in groups, is a paradox rooted in our fundamental nature as we shall see in the following chapter.

Neither Americans nor the English are unique in complaining about the shocks of life in a strange land. All humans in such circumstances experience similar problems and complain about them too. While these challenges are real, we risk an imbalanced view if we do not at the same time note that many people do come to value their experiences in other worlds with other people; they have stimulating and relatively painless experiences. Nevertheless, we learn much by meeting head-on the widespread problems inherent in adjusting to and understanding other lifeways based on different principles. By confronting these issues we learn more about ourselves as well as others, because culture contact necessarily involves two cultures.

In the remainder of this chapter we shall examine some common experiences of culture shock reported by anthropologists. Arranged by some basic categories under the general label of "shocks to the system," we use these shocks to help us to understand the personal side of experience in another culture. In the course of this examination, we discover some of the common challenges the outsider faces and develop a preliminary appreciation of the hold that culture has on each of us.

SHOCKS TO THE SYSTEM

The situations in which people find themselves as they grapple initially with cultural differences range from the humorous and merely embarrassing to the dangerous and emotionally devastating. Barbara Anderson (1990) tells a number of amusing stories of her misadventures in the field, including a hilarious description of being completely flustered in a bath house because of her ignorance of local customs.

Napoleon Chagnon (1992) arrived at a village in the Amazon Basin to be greeted by Yanomamo warriors with spears poised menacingly, their faces smeared with green nasal discharge as a result of taking hallucinogenic drugs. Jean Briggs (1970) spent time with a small group of Inuit (Eskimo) feeling very much out of place and exhibiting a generous measure of emotional volatility, which is not the Inuit way. Her inability to conceal her emotions threatened to disrupt their small group harmony. Although most people will not encounter these extremes in their travels, such examples serve to underscore in dramatic ways some of the issues we will tackle in this text.

Challenges to the Senses

Each cultural place is characterized by a distinct profile of sensory experiences that can please or irritate the senses of a visitor. As Barbara Anderson puts it:

> Unlike our overeager brains, our senses remained resistant and disbelieving in the face of Taarnby's new reality. They clung persistently to a learned logic about the proper sources of bodily comfort. We were never oblivious to the smell of the sea. . . . Unprepared taste buds programmed for different foods, scorned all efforts—mine especially—to adapt to the enjoyment of eel or beer soup. Even my nose resisted odors that, I was later to understand, distinguish villages everywhere and become as encoded and subliminally distinctive of a particular community as a DNA profile of a person. (1990:35)

Writing of her stay in Botswana (in Southeastern Africa), Marianne Alverson notes:

> There is a certain strong, acrid smell impossible to ignore. It is by far the worst odor around here; body odor. I think it is caused by sweating into dirty clothes which absorb the smoke of the evening fire. Nevertheless, we sit close together and pass the kadi (beer); and in the process, we have managed to get used to the smell of poverty. (1987:21)

Alverson's case supports the view that North Americans generally are uncomfortable with body odor and tend to associate it with weakness of moral character and personal slovenliness. Alverson, of course, does not make this association. In an environment of tropical heat and persistent drought, the Tswana have little choice. Human and animal consumption of water warrant first priority. Wearing clothes, a cultural value introduced by Westerners accustomed to a temperate climate, is of questionable value in the tropical environment of the Tswana. Often, one of the first acts of Western domination was to put clothing on native people. Wearing clothing raises costly problems of maintenance and replacement that were not a part of native adaptation to the area. We, on the other hand, are accustomed to an extravagant use of water. Taking baths or showers each day as most North Americans do habitually would be an unthinkable waste in such a dry region. These examples suggest that the term "cultural place" is a good descriptive term, because the characteristic odors emanate from the interaction of culture and nature, both physically and conceptually, in the local place.

In another incident, the Alversons were uncomfortable with the large swarms of flies that hovered constantly about them and their compound in certain seasons of the year. Their host replied to their complaint:

> Certainly there are many flies! Flies mean cattle. If there are many flies in the Lolwapa [compound], a man is said to be rich with cattle. It is no good to destroy flies, or harm will come to the herd. When the herd moves on, so too will the flies. (Alverson 1987:390)

We associate flies with dirt and disease, while the Tswana consider them to be a desirable sign of wealth, because they are mainly cattle herders. Americans certainly are not unfamiliar with flies, but the unrelenting swarms that engulfed the Alversons were a nuisance partly because they were negatively valued by the Americans who tend to associate them with disease. We take for granted our interpretations of what we sense until challenged by contrary interpretations.

Most new sensory experiences become absorbed quickly into a new routine, although some may remain as lingering irritants. In part, this adjustment follows a desensitization through sheer repetition; in part, it emerges from our eventual *classification of sensory data* into an ordered and anticipated world. The Alversons reacted automatically to the flies as if they were at home. Although their informant's explanation that flies indirectly indicate wealth might not have changed their basic attitude much, it gave them another perspective to think about. Intellectually, they understood that their reaction was relevant to their home experience, not the Tswana. It was a start. The clouds of flies were thus made a part of the ordered Tswana world which the Alversons sought to enter.

If some of our new sensory experiences challenge us, still others completely escape our perception.

> "The Basarwa will see here that it is your heel in the sand, that it is the heel of the woman who is not bearing a child, but she is still young. The woman walked slowly when the sun was there, he pointed at the sky and continued. The woman walked on a day with very little wind, a day with no rain clouds nearby. She walked from the southwest to the southeast and stopped here for something. She walked past the twig broken by the foot of one in man's shoes who was moving east to west when the sun was higher in the sky. This is the beetle to collect and make poisons for the hunting arrow. The

woman who walked here was not a woman of the thirstland because she had her own food and water. Why would she leave behind a good eating root with water?"

"A good eating root? Where?"

"This here!"

"This?" I pointed to the skimpy vine at the edge of the circle.

"Certainly! It is not enough to see what is on the top of the sand. You must know what is underneath." (Alverson 1987:111–12)

Alverson could neither observe the signs nor read their meaning had she seen them, because she had no experience in doing such things. She could learn this craft from her hosts if she wished, but probably not as well as those who had grown up in the area and learned as second nature to read the sands.

Specialists in human perception have long known that we practice *selective perception*, which means we focus on some parts of our environment while ignoring other parts. We humans are not equipped to give equal attention to all the sensory data that bombard us daily. What guides our perception for the most part is interest and experience. In short, we focus on what is important to us. Reading spoor in the desert is a survival skill for desert dwellers, but completely useless for city dwellers. When entering another culture we learn what part of their environment they are interested in and why.

Handling initial perceptions is an important part of building the competence and the confidence to move on to other challenges. Anthropologists record their experiences from the first day of their arrival in a new culture, and are often surprised, when later they read their daily journal, at how quickly those initial experiences were absorbed into their unconscious routine (Stoller 1989:3–4). Later, we will revisit the meanings people give to their perceptions of taste and sound.

Communicating

Not speaking the local language or speaking it at a beginner's level of competence makes one feel mute, helpless, and dependent. Not having control over language is particularly frustrating to professionals who are accustomed to speaking in their native language at a high level of competence. Having young children with us may add further to our discomfort because they pick up the local language so quickly—they interact easily with other children.

Even with previous language preparation, we are likely to find ourselves hesitant and fumbling, and given to constant rehearsals of what we intend to say. Linguistic disaster lurks always. Barbara Anderson tells of her experience at coffee hour, when, on her departure, she politely told the host how delicious her pastries were, only to learn later that she actually had said to her startled but bemused host that the food was "goddamned good" (1990:98). Martha Ward, having stepped accidentally on a woman's toes during her work on Pohnpei, in the Pacific, apologized by mistakenly blurting out "His canoe is blue" (1989:22). The people we are visiting are likely to appreciate our willingness to learn their language because the effort validates the worth of their language, but the effort may place us between the horns of a dilemma. On the one hand, if we get a few phrases correct people might leap to the unwarranted conclusion that we know more than we do and slip into their normal speed and style of delivery. On the other hand, over-confidence on our part might be a problem. Moritz Thomsen, a Peace Corps worker, describes the following event.

> Another example of my facility with Spanish: in Ecuador an introduction is a rather formal moment. You are presented to a Ecuadorian, who nicely says that he is absolutely enchanted to meet you and that he is at your service—*a sus ordenes*. For months I simply acknowledged these gracious speeches of pleasure by mumbling over and over, "*mucho gusto Senior, mucho gusto.*" But later, bloated with a self-confidence that had no basis in reality, I began to reply with a few gracious comments of my own, *a su servicio*, I would say smiling brightly and shaking my new friend's hand. "a su servicio," at your service. Someone drew me aside one day and pointed out very discreetly that if I were saying anything at all, I was only offering a toast, "here's to your bathroom," and that in many cases, particularly if the man had no bathroom, I might conceivably be treading on some sensitive nerve endings. (1969:62)

Not only is this a fine case of "bloated self-confidence," but also a good example of the need to acquire a second level of competence in the social connotations of the words we learn to speak.

Laura Bohannan (writing as Elenore Smith Bowen) writes of the confusion between her and her informants:

> It was Accident who made me see the difficulty. As he talked, I again realized that learning the language and learning the culture were mutually dependent. I had misunderstood because I did not know the full social implications of the words. ([1954] 1964:110)

> They did not grasp the nature of my difficulty. Like everyone else, they assumed that if I used a word at all, I must be fully aware of all that it implied. ([1954] 1964:111)

Developing a sensitivity to speech behavior in varying social contexts is often important. Ward (1989:78), for example, had to deal with "honorific" and routine levels of speaking. That is, she had to learn to speak one way to the titled social elite and another to communicate with commoners on a daily basis. Most cultures are socially differentiated in various ways, and language nuances are often geared to these differences. Language performance, then, is sensitive to social and situational contexts in ways that may not be immediately apparent to the outsider.

The sharpened attention we give to speaking and translating in an unfamiliar language is tiring. Add to this essential task the constant pressure of being on stage and subject to critical scrutiny, and one can easily understand how entering another culture can be a fatiguing, albeit rewarding, experience.

Interpreting body language can be an equally treacherous adventure because much of it is not universal, but culture bound. In North America, beckoning someone is accomplished by waving someone to you with elbow down, hand up, palm toward you, and the hand moved as if pulling the person to you. In Ecuador, it is customary to put palm down, elbow to side, and wave as if signalling, from our point of view, someone to go away. Thus, situations arise where an Ecuadorian is verbally telling you to "come here," while simultaneously motioning you "to go away." The visitor is apt to stand frozen to the spot while the Ecuadorian intensifies her attempt to get you to come to her.

Elizabeth Hahn gives an example of misreading body language in Tonga, an island of the Pacific. Visiting a Tongan bureaucrat early in her fieldwork:

> I was having my first "anthropological" discussion—one professional to another. And then it happened—in the middle of one of my explanations, he started raising and wiggling his eyebrows at me. I was taken completely off guard and stammered to a stop. He stopped. No sooner had I resumed talking than he started giving me the eye again. We started and stopped several times. I began to get very angry. There he was looking so innocent with a quizzical expression on his face, as if I were the one doing something odd. How dare he come on to me? (1990:73)

Completely baffled by wiggling eyebrows, Hahn compounds the problem by attributing to the bureaucrat, himself puzzled at the halting flow of conversation, a motive understandable in our culture. She assumes that he has made a fully conscious decision to act in a particular manner, when he is actually performing habitual, and therefore mostly unconscious, behavior. He has no idea why she is acting so peculiarly. She learns later that such eyebrow action is the Tongan equivalent of "uh huh," or "I hear you"—in other words a conversational lubricant.

Ward (1989:72) also learned quickly that in Pohnpei a high-status person should not touch the head of a child because the head of a lower-status person is vulnerable to a flow of power from the higher status person, resulting in injury. A variation in this belief is found throughout Latin America where it is thought that if a higher-status person stares directly at a child he can induce sickness in the child.

Social Use of Food

Choices of food are both personal and cultural and frequently difficult to change, because we become so accustomed to a particular diet. In general, North Americans are not organ eaters. Inuit eat raw seal, but even North American consumers of rare steak want it cooked some. Native peoples find a good source of protein in insects and grubs. In the Orient, cats and dogs are fair game, while for us they are household pets. Some peoples eat eel and snakes. The cattle herders of East Africa drink raw milk mixed with blood drawn from their cattle. The banana-like plantain, to North Americans quite bland with the consistency of cork when heated, is the valued bread of much of South America. Others would find some of our food equally repugnant.

In areas of scarce resources, eating the entire animal is a matter of survival, and good taste. In other words, peoples who consume all of the beast because it may be a matter of survival does not mean that they do not also find it enjoyable. A group may eat all that it can in one sitting. Only by living with such people can we appreciate their motivation.

> Both of us ate ravenously, ignoring the children who gathered to watch the performance. I could feel my stomach distending as I forced more and more food into it. It was a habit we had learned since our arrival. When there is food, eat as much as you can. You never know when you will eat again. A couple of lean days had persuaded us of the truth of this unspoken aphorism. Today we had the sensation which the Sherente cherish and which is much celebrated in their stories: the pleasure of feeling our bellies grow big with food. (Maybury-Lewis [1965] 1988:52)

Not to eat the entire animal would seem to the Sherente a ridiculous waste of food. After all they had no way of storing it, nor any knowledge of when they would kill another animal. Even if we come to eat the local food routinely, we still may be driven to search for ice cream in Ecuador, a fast food outlet in Cairo, Chinese cuisine in Nairobi, Kenya, or pizza in Indonesia. Anthropologists are known to take certain treasured foods, such as peanut butter, into the field with them where they hoard them. By these efforts we attempt to recover the familiar and comfortable, to seal ourselves off as Bohannan comments in the beginning of this chapter, however momentarily, from the other culture. Note what Janet Siskind says about her experience:

> At times when I found life at Marcos frustrating and lonely, I revenged myself childishly by eating crackers and jam in my *mosquitero* [mosquito netting hung over a bed], opening the large can as

quietly as possible since children can hear a cracker can opening over an incredible distance. Despite my caution someone would come by and ask what I was doing. I would reply that I was reading, though no one believed me. Giving and receiving food are important emotion-laden interactions at Marcos. Eating with people is an affirmation of kinship. Refusing to share food is a denial of all relationships, a statement that the other is an outsider. When people are eating and offer nothing, one feels more than hunger, one feels alien and alienated. (Siskind 1973:9)

In Siskind's situation, to lie is the lesser evil. It is a social fiction shared with her neighbors so that she not be considered antisocial in their terms. Had she been a relative and they found out that she was hoarding food, there would have been considerable tension if not serious conflict.

Food, as Siskind notes, is a form of social communication. Who eats with whom and under what circumstances is a statement about social relationships. Even those human groups living the simplest technological existence, the San of the Kalahari Desert of South Africa, for example, have rules of food distribution and consumption that are determined mostly by kinship distance from the hunter most responsible for the kill. Such rules express expectations of sharing in routine ways and reduce potential sources of group conflict. They make a statement about community life.

In a quarter of Marrakech, residents tell Elizabeth Fernea that they did not understand why she and her husband were constantly having dinner guests. They could not decide what was going on because Moroccan custom is to have social dinners only at ceremonial times such as weddings and funerals. As one informant put it ". . . it isn't our custom to have people for dinner just for fun" ([1976] 1988:344). Similarly, when the Ferneas were asked to dinner by Omar, who was better acquainted with Western ways and with Elizabeth's husband, Robert, the neighbors could not understand his purpose. There appeared to be no ceremonious occasion. When the Ferneas arrived at Omar's, they ate alone as is the custom. Only after the meal was finished, hands washed, and tea served, did the host family join them. They seemed caught between two worlds; on the one hand they were invited to Omar's counter to custom, but were entertained according to local custom for rare, nonceremonious visitors.

Understandings about the distribution and consumption of food are culturally shaped so early in life that they are taken as a natural state of affairs. In the following example, both parties commit the fallacy of naive realism, the unconscious assumption that some acts are so basic and simple that they always carry the same meaning across cultures.

There are still patterns of past social interaction which I engage in without thinking. It is only when they are inappropriate that I even

> become aware of them. Here a host does not question visitors as to
> their preference. After all there is no choice. If kadi has been
> brewed, the beer must be offered. If there is no kadi, tea is cooked
> and served. When serving, a host does not ask visitors whether they
> wish a refill, for to a Tswana, such questioning reveals a lack of gen-
> erosity and true friendship. (Alverson 1987:52)

Alverson kept asking her visitors, to their chagrin, if they wanted refills.
She was perplexed by the increasingly tense atmosphere. Beneath this
tension lay those naive and hidden assumptions on both sides that certain acts of hospitality are so fundamental to human nature, they should
be easily understood by everyone. Yet both parties are challenged by puz-
zling words and facial expressions which indicate that something is
wrong. In this case, their willingness to discuss the confusion resulting
from this "simple," but culturally defined, act of hospitality helped each
party to discover something important about both themselves and the
other. Hahn's encounter with the bureaucrat in Tonga, the one who wig-
gled his eyebrows, is another example of naive realism.

Customs dedicated to giving or receiving, whether service or food,
present to the unwary outsider another hazard on the road to adjustment. David Counts tells of his experience in Papua, New Guinea, where
he managed to shame his village host by purchasing watermelon. The
emotionally painful event led him to the following conclusion: "In a society where food is shared or gifted as part of social life, you may not buy it
with money" (1990:20). Later, he was overwhelmed with gifts of bananas
and tried to refuse additional stalks, an act which immediately brought a
return visit from his already embarrassed host. This time his host
admonished him by saying that if he had more stalks than he could eat,
he should give some to his visitors. Counts learned a second lesson.
"Never refuse a gift, and never fail to return a gift. If you cannot use it,
you can always give it away to someone else—there is no such thing as
too much—there are never too many bananas" (1990:22). His final lesson:
"where reciprocity is the rule and gifts are the idiom, you cannot demand
a gift, just as you cannot refuse a gift" (1990:24). Although not claiming a
scholarly conclusion regarding universal rules of reciprocity—these are,
in fact, very common ideas cross-culturally—Counts nevertheless demonstrates his wish to uncover the cultural principles of giving and receiving
necessary to guide him in his future interactions in New Guinea.

Cultural expectations about giving and receiving are important
because the circumstances of exchange are statements about social relationships, and to violate the rules of exchange is therefore to violate the
standards of normative social interaction. It is important for an outsider
to acquire an early grasp of these rules.

Gender Roles

Being an outsider has both costs and benefits. When we hear of an outsider being inducted into a clan or tribe, we tend to think that the person is being honored. Indeed, outsiders are so honored on occasion. But it is more likely that the outsider is simply being placed in a familiar role in the local social structure in order to define how local people will interact with her. An outsider role is awkward and confusing because it carries no familiar expectations guiding social interaction. Siskind (1973:15) notes that her work with informants among the Sharanahua of Peru was difficult and tense because she fit no existing role in their society. Dumont ([1978] 1992) tried to behave in a manner designed to prevent his Panare hosts from classifying him in various outsider roles. He drank some alcohol, for example, to avoid being classified as a Christian missionary. But, when one of his informants made him a brother, he wondered if he and the Panare meant the same thing by the term. Was he a literal or a figurative brother? The new classification did succeed in giving him somewhat of an insider status and, as a result, improved the Panares' behavior toward him, as well as his toward them. Still, he remained unconvinced of the answer to his question.

Being an outsider sometimes gives one some freedom of movement not accorded to male and female insiders, and we can sometimes negotiate other dispensations as Oboler managed during her time with the Nandi of Kenya (1986). Being an outsider rarely, however, exempts one completely from the expectations of the host culture. Oboler and her husband had to forget about some of their behavior as an American husband and wife, such as holding hands while walking together in public (1986:39). The woman's role among the Nandi is to walk behind the husband, and Oboler could negotiate no dispensation in this case.

In urban settings where people are accustomed to outsiders there is more freedom to act and less pressure to "fit in." The limits of familiar roles can be expanded and new roles more easily introduced. The influence of mass media, the rise of a technocrat class, and modernization generally tend to make people more receptive to change. The face-to-face relationship so important to social control in small communities is missing.

Sometimes, forced changes are more subtle. Alverson reports this comment from her husband:

"I know its been hard on you," he admitted.

"We're living on top of each other in this hut, yet we're in separate worlds. Haven't you noticed? We have become a Tswana couple. The men talk to men. The women talk to women. Sometimes they mix, but usually in private, usually in the still of the night." (1987:188)

The Ferneas had a similar experience with social pressures in Morocco. Women are confined to the private domestic realm and the company of other women, while men operate mostly in the public domain among other men.

Both men and women face restrictions on their attempts to gather data from the opposite sex. Segregation of gender role behavior in societies operating under heavy Arab and Islamic cultural influence raises intriguing questions about how a female anthropologist could study effectively any cultural domain other than that of women. Altorki and El-Sohl (1984) assembled a number of reports from Arab women who worked in Arab culture as Ph.D. anthropologists. They concluded that while there are definite problems, their success depended more on the contingencies of time, place, and the nature of the problem being investigated than on the inflexibility of gender identity. In general, women have been more successful than men in crossing gender domains for productive study.

There is always a tension between being deeply involved and trying to escape some of the social constraints imposed by another culture. Anthropologists face the dilemma of being "marginal natives" (Freilich 1968), of trying to be on the inside while knowing that they will always be essentially outsiders. We want it both ways. Jean Briggs (1970) was "made" a daughter, which delighted her until she discovered that she was expected to act like a daughter, and do the work of a daughter. Suddenly, her privileged status was in jeopardy. Laura Bohannan comments:

> I had longed to be accepted, but I meant something rather different
> by it: the privilege of going my own way with their full confidence.
> Udama now pointed out that I could not at the same time claim the
> guest's privilege of doing more or less as I wished and the family
> privilege of going behind the scenes. ([1954] 1964:123)

Bohannan elected to go behind the scenes, to participate, but still had trouble with her anthropological conscience to observe, which in turn interfered with her participation. Experienced anthropologists know, as Bohannan did, that productive fieldwork is based on achieving an artful balance between observation and participation. We need to be a part of the community we study, yet free to withdraw when we think we need to for reasons of personal adjustment or maintaining a degree of objectivity. Sometimes, anthropologists are caught between rival factions and find it necessary therefore to maintain some distance from issues. Degree and conditions of participation are continuing quandaries of fieldwork.

Age and sex are universal characteristics by which to define role and status obligations and rights. Learning role and status, perhaps beginning with the family, is a good way of uncovering the expectations and etiquette of social interaction. Outsiders then face Bohannan's quandary of how much of their own culture they will give up, how much

they will retain. Cultures differ in how lenient they are with those outsiders who do not wish to modify their behavior.

Moral Dilemmas

Living in another culture is an instructive exercise in values clar-
ification. Encountering strange behavior and disparate beliefs will
challenge our ideas about what is important in human affairs. We cannot completely avoid these tests even on the tourist circuit, but any
serious effort to engage another culture on its own terms is sure to raise
many moral issues. Most of these dilemmas will be ultimately unresolv-
able for the outsider, unless she is prepared to take great risks in
advocating change.

Elizabeth Fernea ([1976] 1988:103–4) describes her concern for a
man lying in the street covered with blood and dirt. She hesitated in the
street wondering if she should help and speculating about the extent of
his injuries. Why was he lying there unattended with a police station a
mere block away? As she stood, trying to read the cultural significance
of the scene before her, a man behind her said to her in French to move
on; it was none of her affair. That evening she and her husband, Bob,
speculated further on how to read this incident. Was it because she was
a foreigner? A woman? Was the injured man drunk? Was his family
close by and on their way to aid him? She does not report whether they
ever discovered the reason.

Effective action depends on an accurate reading of the situation.
When the outsider does not have a clue as to the cultural significance
underlying an observed event, she does not know the appropriate action
to take. Anthropologists use such mysteries to help them dig deeper into
local life ways. But it is critical to remember that it is not just the other
culture that is under examination here, but the outsider's as well. Colin
Turnbull makes this comparison explicit with respect to the treatment
of animals among the Mbuti:

> At other times I have seen Pygmies singeing feathers off birds that
> were still alive, explaining that the meat is tender if death comes
> slowly. And the hunting dogs, valuable as they are, get kicked
> around mercilessly from the day they are born to the day they die.
> I have never seen any attempt to domesticate any animal or bird
> apart from the hunting dog. When I talked to the Pygmies about
> their treatment of animals, they laughed at me and said, "The for-
> est has given us animals for food—should we refuse the gift and
> starve?" I thought of turkey farms and Thanksgiving, and of the
> millions of animals reared in our own society with the sole intention
> of slaughtering them for food. (Turnbull 1962:100)

North Americans have their own dichotomous categories of animals as
pets, and animals as food. Our values are shaped on the one hand by

romanticized and anthropomorphized stories of animals in our media, and, on the other hand, by the fact that we are no longer accustomed to working animals. Some would say that we commit our own form of savagery on experimental laboratory animals for our benefit.

Alverson's (1987) young son began to develop his own ideas about cultural differences, his and the Tswana's, in the treatment of animals.

> "Moremi is—cruel—to the goats. He wouldn't let the limping goat stay in the Kraal. He pushed it out. He made it go on. I tried to stop him. He laughed. He beat it. He kept the baby goat away from its mother. It wanted to drink. He wouldn't let it. Why is he so mean? He never pets them." (p. 25)

> "I know why Moremi doesn't name my goats. People are hungry here. A goat is meat," he said simply. (p. 31)

North Americans do not usually name goats, turkeys, and beef cows either. They also are in the category of food.

North Americans are often angered and frustrated by another culture's poor health conditions which seem simple enough to combat.

> I had very complicated feelings about this child. My relationship with the family was strained on her account. At mealtime, with the baby sleeping on the floor or eating pieces of bananas or rice off the floor, I would get so mad, and so mad at my anger and my inability to function, that I couldn't speak. We had had many discussions about the child's nutrition, some of them quite intense and sarcastic. Maybe they *did* have good native herbs for treating their sickness, but I kept telling them that with decent nutrition the child would grow and maintain a degree of health. (Thomsen 1969:53)

More often than not, fieldworkers muddle through these dilemmas without resolving them in their own mind, or without effecting any lasting changes—which is not usually their purpose anyway. North Americans like to solve "needless" problems that would appear to have simple solutions if we could just get "them" to think like we do. Anthropologists sometimes feel that way too, but tend to be cautious about suggesting change because they may not have the "whole picture" and because they generally believe that the people themselves must want to change to make change effective. Also, change sometimes has unfortunate and unforeseen ramifications that negate positive change.

Laura Bohannan speaks of the tragedy of witchcraft accusation.

> I too had begun to tremble. Here it was no comfort that witches were only people. Therein lay the tragedy. These men were torn with anguish, striving to save the life of one they loved. Amara could yet live, if they could only force a confession from the witch. Each knew himself innocent. Each therefore knew the other guilty. I knew them both innocent. I watched while each strove to break

the other, to force his confession, to save Amara. I knew they could
not. Their battle was the more terrible for me because it was in vain
and fought against shadows. ([1954] 1964:193)

There was nothing that Bohannan could do or say in this dilemma, but
try to cope with her own emotions.

Belmonte found himself searching for answers to his discomfort
with the level of violence he discovered in lower-class Neapolitan families.

Reliving the confused events of an afternoon as I wrote up my field
notes became a wrenching chore. How could I record yet another exchange of insults, another bout of spitting, another discontinuous
series of pecks and counterpecks? I began to block out sections of
my notebook with the simple exclamation, "chaos!" which meant
that the scene had flown out of control and I could no longer follow
the flail of arms and fists, and the twisted, wincing faces, the curs-
es, the grunts and the cries. (1989:79)

At times, Belmonte avoided visiting the family because he could not
handle the level of violence displayed there, but at the same time he
wondered if they felt that he had abandoned them because of who they
were. These are problems not usually solved in any satisfactory way but
linger with the outsider even after he has left the scene.

INTRACULTURAL JOLTS

There is sufficient diversity within any reasonably large-scale society to produce jolts, if not shocks. For example, Tannen's (1990) work
shows how males and females of the same culture, using the same language, talk past each other. They do so because gender differences
shape their experience in the larger cultural world in dissimilar ways.
As a consequence, the same words take on different meanings according
to gender. In addition to gender, divergence of experience may be fos-
tered by variables of age, social class, religious membership, urban or
rural location, ethnicity, geographical region, or occupation, to mention
a few. Performing different jobs within an organization of any kind can
produce small worlds of difference which sometimes seem almost
insurmountable.

People are often more inclined to be tolerant, perhaps unaccompa-
nied by understanding, of other ways of life outside their own culture,
but less so of subcultural differences in their own. Distance somehow
seems to make it safer to be understanding, while at the same time you
can better ignore whatever they do that you don't like. We might even
think that people in our culture ought to know better, and we give them

less room for difference. Nonetheless, the same principles for understanding cultural difference apply to intracultural difference.

CONCLUSION

These examples of culture shock illustrate our struggle to extend ourselves beyond the world we have created to comprehend a world created by others. We regard our sensory perceptions, language, social use of food, gender roles, and morality to be natural and fundamental to our way of life. Yet, they are likely to be among the first elements to be threatened as we experience another culture. The confrontation between "their" way and "our" way causes us to reflect on our differences. Differences may be overwhelming at first and impede our progress toward recognizing similarities. Differences are real and cannot be ignored, but common ground can still be discovered.

The experience of culture shock reveals to us two realities of human nature:
1. We live a life highly *bound* by our local cultural experience.
2. We cross our local cultural border with difficulty, but it can be crossed.

This book is about our experience, their experience, and building bridges that span the difference.

Chapter Two

Common Ground

We seem endlessly torn between the one opinion that beneath our obviously diverse ways all human groups are really the same and the contrary opinion that we are, in fact, as truly different as we appear to be. Anthropologists working in exotic cultures recognize the familiar even as they struggle to make sense of the strange. They despair of really comprehending another culture even as they write scientific reports on their current state of understanding. The truth is that human groups *are* fundamentally the *same*, but *also* vitally *different*. The familiar coexists with the strange. This complex reality requires that we develop a balanced view of humanity that takes into account both its universal similarities and its exotic local expressions.

Developing a comprehensive framework of cultural similarities and differences has been the continuing task of anthropology, and it is one of the principal goals of this text. This chapter presents the first part of the framework devoted to establishing our common humanity, while the following chapter is dedicated to grasping the genesis of local differences. In the present chapter we will address our common biological heritage and physical variation, the concept of culture, human thought and emotions, and ways of controlling or channeling human behavior.

We cannot properly address issues of human diversity unless we first know who we are as a species, and thereby locate our common ground. To accomplish this task, we need to acquire a firm grasp of the evolutionary basis of human behavior and potential. Acquiring a firm grasp means, in this case, answering some key questions, from a comparative point of view, regarding the essential bases of cultural life. Do human groups differ in intelligence? Do some groups have superior sensory equipment? Do we all have the same emotions? How is a human self formed? What role does morality play in our lives? What role does our lived experience play in shaping our culture? How are individuals connected to groups? What is the concept of culture and how does it lead us to better insight into ourselves and others?

BRAIN, MIND, AND EVOLUTION

Compared to other animals, all normal humans are characterized by an exceptional ability to *learn*, an unparalleled faculty for *complex communication*, and a unique capacity for *self-awareness*. Although the story of how we came to possess these qualities is too long and complex to tell in detail here, an abbreviated account will suffice to record a few critical developments in our evolutionary past and to note their consequences for the kind of creature we have come to be.

The critical evolutionary developments are three: (1) achieving upright posture, (2) increasing the size and complexity of the brain, and (3) acquiring language. Although it remains unclear precisely what evolutionary pressures caused the emergence of bipedalism, it is clear that *Australopithecines* (prehumans found only in Africa) had achieved an upright posture by three to four million years ago. Whether upright posture was favored by a new capacity to make tools with freed hands or by a new ability to see over the tall grass of East Africa to search for stalking predators is not clear. A combination of these and still other unidentified forces may have formed us as bipedal creatures. What is clear is that the ability to stand on two legs preceded brain expansion and the acquisition of speech.

The second critical development was an increase in brain size, accompanied by the appearance of an expanded cerebral cortex, which is the outer layer of the brain and the home of higher brain functions. The brain capacity of *Australopithecines* did not exceed about 475 cc, while the brain capacity of *Homo erectus*, who succeeded them, is known to run from about 775 cc. to 1200 cc, or about 1000 cc on the average. This is significantly larger than the earlier *Australopithecine* brains. The upper range of *Homo erectus* brain capacity reached nearly to the lower range of modern capacities of approximately 1200 cc. to 1800 cc. Thus, fossil skulls from the *Homo erectus* era (about 500,000 to 1.6 million years ago) are much more vaulted than earlier forms in order to contain the larger brain.

Frontal expansion, cranial vaulting, and the impressions left by the brain on the underside of the skull plates record the development of the cerebral cortex. Besides being the site of higher brain functions, the cortex is responsible for initiating the complex code that instructs us to push air past the pharynx to produce the sounds that eventually are molded into speech. The expansion of the brain, clearly present in *Homo erectus* and the acquisition of complex communication skills, perhaps beginning at this same time, dramatically increased our ability to learn. By the time that *Neanderthals* appeared on the scene over 100,000 years ago, brain capacities matched or exceeded the modern range. *Cro-Magnon*, the first modern human, arrived by 40,000 years ago, exhibiting fully human form and function. All human groups living today share the same brain structure and chemistry because we all derived from a common ancestor.

These developments opened us to endless possibilities. As Campbell (1987:343) puts it:

> Language we can see now, was humankind's passport to a totally new level of social relationship, organization, and thought; it was the tool that allowed humans to vary expressions to meet changing conditions instead of being limited by less flexible patterns of communication, as other primates are.

The system of communication used by our closest primate relatives, chimpanzees, is a *signal*, or *call*, system. Call systems are closed systems that are largely restricted to signals of danger and to involuntary expressions of internal emotional and physiological states (Campbell 1987:342). They are not modified or expanded by experience over the generations.

Language, on the other hand, is an open system that can be expanded as experience and learning require. All human groups possess a language that is perfectly adequate to the challenges of their local neighborhood and can be adapted and expanded to changing conditions. There are no inferior or superior languages; they do what they are intended to do. In prehistoric times, language use would have supported and enhanced more complex social cooperation, thus improving our ancestors' chances for survival.

Displacement is the feature of language that allows us to speak about those conditions and objects that are not immediately observable to us. Through language we can displace ourselves in time and place—as this text does. Displacement means that we can dwell on our memories and plan for the future; we can think and talk about ourselves as will be, or have been. We can speak of faraway places. Our capacity for abstract thought allows us to be *reflective* creatures, aware of ourselves as individuals and as members of a group. The physical evolution of the brain and the development of language, then, are accompanied by an evolution of consciousness.

One critically important consequence of our evolutionary development is our increasing reliance on learning. Instead of starting off early in life with the full complement of survival behaviors generally characteristic of immature mammals, humans must learn to be competent adults over a long period of maturation. We are not "hard-wired" for rigid, specific response behaviors but learn from experience to modify behavior as needed. Other creatures can learn from experience, too, but are relatively restricted in this respect. Different challenges in different times and places demand that we learn new lessons as we adapt.

We learn what we need to learn in order to survive in a particular natural and cultural environment, and this is as true today as it was millennia ago when, as fledgling humans, we first faced the ultimate problem of physical survival under harsh and demanding circumstances. We evolved as tropical creatures yet we spread rapidly into nearly every climatic region in the world.

Today, we face equally challenging problems of how we are to survive the consequences of those early successes. Clearly, one of the lessons we have not learned so well is how to get along with each other. A key element in dispelling myth and prejudice is to appreciate the universal role of experience and interest, however different, in shaping human perceptions, thoughts, and feelings.

SOCIAL RACE

Cultural difference is not based on racial difference. There is no innate relationship between race and behavior or values. Various forms of prejudice and discrimination frequently posit relationships between race and intelligence and morality, but these are sociological issues. *Social race* refers to the fact that people use culturally and socially constructed labels to identify groups thought to be races. As Kottak (1994:77) observes, a child born of a mixed black and white marriage in North America will be arbitrarily labeled black, although that label does not fit biological reality. In North America, one is either black or white; in Brazil, there are many categories between these polar opposites, thus recognizing various shades of mixture. They too are arbitrary categories with little meaning except for what people want to make of them sociologically.

Humans no doubt have been aware of physical differences as long as they have existed. Whether perceived differences had any particular meaning for early humans is unknown. Throughout much of history, cultural and religious differences appear to have been more important than differences in physical appearance. The *extensive* and *systematic* racism, with themes of innate and fixed superiority and inferiority, that we observe in the world today and in our recent past appears to have been linked with the rise of colonialism in the West.

The act of classifying requires establishing criteria by which to sort phenomena into classes. The common criteria used by Westerners for centuries to sort humans into racial categories were skin color, nose form, hair form, shape of the skull, and height. In their eagerness to achieve their scientific mission of describing cultures and peoples of the world, anthropologists at one time also used these criteria, but without the assumption of fixed and inherited ability. In the 1960s, however, anthropologists became increasingly wary of racial classification and ceased constructing their own classifications. There are a number of reasons for becoming uneasy about racial classification.

One reason for scientific discomfort is that the commonly used criteria do not present themselves to us in neat packages as stereotypes suggest. Knowing the skin color of a group tells us nothing with certainty about its hair or nose form. If one were to map independently each criterion as it appears around the world, much like the clinal variations in temperature on a weather map, one would observe areas of overlap among traits, but also large areas where they do not covary. We would be better off predicting the weather from the variables of temperature and barometric pressure than we would predicting a racial stereotype. Making such a map of racial traits is called *clinal analysis*, and the resulting mismatch of popular racial traits—independent variation rather than covariation—is known as *discordance*. Some native peoples in the western desert of Australia, for example, have very dark skin, but blonde, or "tawny," hair. Clinal analysis undermines racial stereotyping.

A second problem is that there is little demonstrated scientific reason for designing a racial classification, even for biological or medical reasons. We know that darker skin provides superior protection against skin cancer (because it filters out harmful ultraviolet rays) and that taller, thinner people survive better in the desert, while shorter and more compactly built people do better in the Arctic (because of their differential ability to dissipate or conserve heat). These are cases of climatic engineering providing us with clues for the manufacture of difference. But we quickly run out of other reasons for classification. African-Americans and Africans, particularly from West Africa, display a high incidence, 25 percent to 40 percent in some areas, of sickle-cell anemia (oxygen-starved red blood cells become misshapen, and infected people die early in life if untreated), but so do some Mediterranean European populations (as well as those in other geographical regions). A study of this illness would cut across European, African, and African-American populations.

A third argument against racial classification is that it assumes the existence of pure races, which in fact probably has never been true. It should be noted too that there has never been any solid evidence that blending races has any deleterious effect; if anything, the result of interracial marriage is that it usually produces children of ability equal to or superior to that of the parents. In any case, racial mixture has been common since ancient times.

Finally, racial grouping is always being tied improperly to questions of intelligence and morality as shown in the following section. The failure to distinguish among race, culture, language, and religion leads to confusion even with the best of intentions. Yet these characteristics, like racial traits, vary independently of each other. We are left with the question of why we would want to classify, for what purpose? What have we learned by such an operation? The answer is that we are motivated to make those arbitrary cultural classifications for reasons covered by the concept of social race, that is, for sociological reasons. Increasingly, then, anthropologists do not accept the biological reality of race, viewing it solely as a cultural construction.

THOUGHT, EMOTIONS, AND CULTURE

Perception and Cognition

The key to understanding perception and cognition cross-culturally lies in acquiring a knowledge of how a people are socialized to think about their social and natural environment. *Perception refers to the process of receiving and organizing sensory data at a primary level.* All human groups are bound by the same physical universe of sensations. We do not see ultraviolet rays, or hear a dog whistle, and we have a comparatively poor sense of smell, but we are literally driven by our intelligence to make sense of what we do perceive. We are intellectually aggressive; we reach out to seize nature and to organize it conceptually in a manner that makes sense to us. What makes sense to a specific group of people is to be found in their local experience.

Outsiders, by definition, initially lack the requisite knowledge to understand local perceptions, but often make their ethnocentric judgments anyway. Early European explorers, colonial administrators, and missionaries lacked knowledge of the peoples they contacted, but this ignorance usually did not prevent them from making unenlightened judgments. Moreover, they often had little real interest in discovering the "native view," and thus tended to end their sojourns as bound by their own world as if they had never sailed the ocean sea. The combination of a Eurocentric attitude toward non-Western peoples and their ignorance of other ways of life generated a number of negative stereotypes of other peoples. Westerners indulged themselves in a number of fallacies such as a belief in the "primitive mind," or a savage "sixth sense." Many believed that native peoples were simply "superstitious children." The latter belief conveniently supported the dominating and paternalistic stance of Westerners toward those whom they subjugated. On the other hand, native peoples have their own ignorance and stereotypes about Westerners. But the brain is the same for all normal humans, while the mind varies as a product of the brain's interaction with experience and culture in specific settings.

Many cross-cultural studies have substantiated the critical role of local experiences in producing different performances on tests of perception and cognition. Anthropologists often cite examples of differences in perception. We have already seen that Alverson failed to read the story of the sands because she had no relevant experience. A native child could read spoor much better than she. On the other hand, her hosts would have equal difficulty functioning in a technologically sophisticated city. Turnbull (1962:263) tells of being accompanied by the forest pygmies to distant savannas. Emerging from the forest, they saw for the first time buffalo grazing in the distance. The pygmies, who had lived their entire lives cloistered by the thick rainforest that envelopes them, asked Turnbull about the curious "insects" in front of them. They could not believe that these buffalo were much larger than they appeared to be because they could not conceptually compensate for the effect of distance on their perception of size. This is not primitive mentality but the work of life experience.

Berry (1976) was able to relate the different performances of Inuit (Eskimos of Baffin Island) and Temne (West Africa) on tests of spatial perception to both the local ecology and child-rearing practices. The Inuit are hunters in a snow-clad environment which, to outsiders, is read as a featureless world of white. They must be able successfully to find their way around this world; they must be acutely aware of fine details. The Inuit train their children for independence by stressing personal skills, self-reliance, and individualism. These child-rearing practices have survival value and correlate generally with a high degree of spatial awareness and visual discrimination. Both perception and child rearing are adaptive, and not a series of random choices.

The Temne, on the other hand, are sedentary farmers surrounded by richly detailed vegetation. Their survival does not depend on making fine distinctions in their natural environment. Temne child-rearing practices stress relationships of dependency, and dependency correlates with less spatial discrimination and awareness. The difference between the two groups is related to significantly different sets of natural challenges and cultural solutions. Cultural differences and perception styles emerge from meeting those challenges. We issue the caveat here that environment does not determine culture, it only limits possibilities, especially where groups have limited technology.

In recent years, two ethnographic studies of the senses have jolted anthropologists into the realization that they have been largely ignorant of how cultures systematically shape sensory data. Stoller's (1989) study of the Songhay of Niger deals more generally with the senses, while Feld's (1990) work is an ethnography of the sound system, both natural and human, of the Kaluli of Papua, New Guinea. Stoller is particularly critical of Western scientific empiricism which "focuses" on the sense of vision, the gaze, as a primary metaphor for knowing. The term observation connotes gazing. He suggests that a historical shift, the scientific revolution and its stress on scientific observation, accounts for this emphasis. However, the principal point here is that Westerners are predisposed to stress the visual while other cultures may stress other senses, as Feld's work on sound demonstrates. We will return to Feld later in this chapter.

Western concepts of linear time and stress on punctuality are not shared necessarily by other cultures. When outsiders and insiders act on the basis of different assumptions about time, misunderstanding and irritation frequently arise. Space, time, and social relationships can merge into one elusive category in some cultures. Laura Bohannan ([1954] 1964:52) was asked to accompany some informants on a visit to relatives. When she asked how long the trip would take in order to know whether to pack a lunch, she was told that it would be some distance. Believing it would be perhaps a half-day's walk, she packed a lunch, only to arrive at their destination in less than an hour. Later, she realized that her informants were speaking in kinship terms of social distance rather than geographical distance. They were "distant" relatives living close. She had not misunderstood what they said, but what they meant—distance measured in social terms.

Cognition is the process of gaining, storing, and using knowledge. Cognition, too, is best understood as shaped by experience and interests. Puzzled by certain test results on stimulus orientation between English and Zambian children, Serpell (1971a, 1971b) devised a culturally sensitive test. Whereas earlier studies revealed no difference in performance on simple stimuli, they did show a difference on stimuli patterns. Curious, Serpell decided to give three separate tasks to the children. Children in both groups were accustomed to modeling clay, and so both were given such a test. Because the Zambian children were also accustomed to wire modeling, and the English children to copying figures with pencil and paper, Serpell added these tasks to the first. Both groups did well on the clay task, with which they had common experience, and each did well on its particular, accustomed task. Neither group, however, did as well as the other on the task that was new to it. Each group performed best on that task with which it had experience, and poorly on the unfamiliar one. This study illustrates the role of experience in processes of cognition.

Cognitive anthropology is devoted to discovering how cultures and subcultures organize, store, and apply their knowledge. A classic ethnography in this vein is Spradley's (1970) work with alcoholics on skid row, where he elicits from his informants their organization of experience centered on drinking and being jailed for public drunkenness. Another example of a cognitive approach is Agar's (1973) study of heroin addicts' organization of a world centered on getting and using heroin. Although these two studies take as their subjects people who are uniquely dedicated to one consuming task, getting and staying drunk or getting and staying high, they bear vivid testimony to the human ability to integrate intellect, experience, and interest and to focus subsequent action. The individuals in these groups are organizing and naming their world for reasons that are important to them. If we can understand what motivates people to act and to organize intellectually their world in a certain way, we can better understand their behavior.

Tests of perception and cognition that were developed in the West have been administered frequently in other cultures with varying results. These tests are, however, quite treacherous when given cross-culturally. It is especially important, first, to understand that they are often given to people with no experience, or particular motivation, in taking such tests. Second, the tests are typically developed and "normed" in one culture and applied in another. Thus they often involve tasks that do not translate well in another culture. Therefore we must be particularly careful about the assumptions behind the tests and the conclusions we draw from their results.

The administration and interpretation of tests cross-culturally should be accompanied by a sound knowledge of the cultural context. Cole and Means (1981:54) point out how daunting it is to discover the variables that explain observed behavior when the experience of the investigators and that of the subjects are significantly different. Any observed behavior can have numerous antecedents. Indeed, Cole makes the same point about intracultural tests of cognition. Even within our own culture we are testing persons of a different age, a different gender, a different social class, or a different ethnic group than that of the researcher. How well does the observer know these worlds? How well does she see their world from their point of view? Devising and interpreting cross-cultural tests is like traversing what appears to be solid common ground only to discover it pitted with pockets of intellectual quicksand.

It is well known by now that standard tests of intelligence are culture bound, and gender and social class biased. They are effective in predicting how well one will do in formal schooling, which is what they were primarily designed to do. As Gould (1981) details in his study of the

development and early use of Binet's intelligence test, the test was born
of practical need realized by the French government to identify those children in public school who required remedial education. It was not an
application flowing from a specific theory of intelligence. It was almost
immediately misused to label negatively those children who did poorly on
it. In North America, it was popularized by H. H. Goddard and Lewis Terman who were interested in showing intelligence to be fixed and
distributed unequally through the population. Popular acceptance of the
test was speeded when R. M. Yerkes launched massive testing of over 1.5
million recruits in World War I. Unfortunately, the results seemed to
indicate that virtually half of the white recruits were functioning morons,
while recent immigrants and blacks did even worse (Gould 1981:223).
Although this finding was due to serious flaws in the test and its application, alarmists, fearing depletion of genetic purity in the United States,
used the results to push through Congress legislation to restrict immigra-
tion, especially from non-Western European countries.

The use of intelligence tests to document innate differences between
various racial and ethnic groups still emerges from time to time in spite
of all the problems they still have. While we cannot here explore fully
their uses and abuses, it should be emphasized that the tests themselves
are influenced by experience, both in their construction and scoring and
in the responses of the subjects who take the test. Gould (1981:176) cites
an example of a question that Terman added to Binet's original list. A
Native American in town for the first time in his life observed a white
man riding down the street. The Native American said that the white
man was lazy for walking sitting down. The question is, what was the
white man riding? Terman only accepted bicycle as the answer—not cars
because the driver's legs did not go up and down, nor horses because a
Native American would know a horse. Nor would he accept a person in a
wheel chair or someone riding on another person's back. Other questions
had to do with cultural items, such as identifying a baseball player, something an immigrant would have difficulty doing.

Whenever they are administered in populations with a different
experience, for example those lacking experience in formal schooling, the
results are likely to be invalid and interpretations suspect. Indeed, the
more Western schooling that non-Western groups have, the better they
do on these tests, because their experience more closely matches the experience upon which the tests are based (Cole et al. 1971). Within our own
culture the single most important variable influencing scores for any
group is the socioeconomic status of the subject's family (Gould 1981).
Finally, individuals vary widely in abilities and aptitudes in any culture,
but there appears to be no significant difference in intellectual ability
among groups cross-culturally.

From this discussion of perception and cognition we can derive two general principles:

1. All humans live in the same perceptual world, and have the same basic cognitive capacity.
2. The specific organization and use of knowledge in a particular culture relates more to the experience, interests, and challenges perceived by the members of that culture than it does to those of another culture.

The second principle suggests a third, one of discovery:

3. We will discover the key to understanding another culture in the experience and interests of that culture.

These principles advance our understanding of similarities and differences because they identify simultaneously our shared inheritance and our lived difference. All groups begin life with the same "equipment," but different experiences in different neighborhoods of the world forge different lifeways and different ways of seeing the world. Still at issue, on the other hand, is just how early and to what degree do cultural experiences begin to mold these basic processes.

Emotions

Culture constructs a world of feelings characteristic of individuals and groups. While specialists disagree over exactly how many emotions humans have, there is a much wider agreement on a common core. Fear is an important emotion because of its ability to warn us of threat and to focus our attention; it has obvious survival value. The feeling of attachment is quite understandable in a social species, and having feelings of attachment necessarily sets us up for the feeling of loss, or grief. Anger is clearly universal. What we call happiness or joy certainly is a candidate. Beyond these universal five, the list becomes more contentious.

We shall take the same perspective on emotions that we did with perception and cognition. We all share a common capacity for a variety of emotions regardless of how they are expressed, valued, or named in a particular culture. There is good evidence (Ekman 1982:128–43) that people from different cultures can read with fair accuracy the display of many emotions registered on the faces of people in other cultures. But much more study is required on this subject before firm conclusions can be reached. We should recall that facial displays and body language fall into the realm of observable behavior; the hard part is guessing what is going on behind the display. Like responses to tests of perception and cognition, the display may have many antecedent causes. The actor, for example, might actually be masking her "true" emotions. Levy (1973:97–98) tells of the distrust that early visitors expressed toward Tahitians because they never knew what they were feeling by looking at their faces. Westerners interpreted Tahitian facial displays as deceptive and the people thus as insincere; the Tahitians, on the other hand, thought it too disruptive to the group to visibly wear one's emotions in public. Social grace and cohesion are valued over personal expressiveness.

One of the major problems in dealing with emotions cross-culturally lies in language translation. The central issue is that we impose the discrete categories of language on what appears to be complex and ambiguous natural phenomena. If we translate emotion words from another language, for example, love and anger, are they different words for the same emotions, or do they in fact denote different emotions? Lutz (1988) offers an example of the problems inherent in translating emotion words. The Ifaluk use the term *fago* to refer to what we might call love. Lutz, however, suggests that the social implications of fago and love are different. Fago does not suggest the primary sexual, romantic aspect that love does in our terms. Instead, fago entails a caring and responsibility, even sadness, for those less fortunate than the giver of fago (p. 119). It suggests a hierarchical relationship not present in our conception of love. She further notes that *song*, justifiable anger, is centered on moral violations of personal relationships (p. 155), while anger in mainstream North American culture arises most often over the constraint and frustration of individuality (p. 231). A strict translation of fago and song into English equivalents would therefore be misleading.

The issue of translation is not simply semantic carping; love and anger really are different in Ifaluk culture. Here we face the question of properly weighing the general against the particular—the question of a balanced perspective mentioned earlier. Which alternative we chose depends on the question being asked. The first question is the universal one: do all humans have the capacity for anger? The answer is clearly yes. The second question has to do with how anger is defined, used, and expressed in a particular culture. The first question addresses our commonality, but it is cast at such a general level of understanding that, while crucial to constructing a basic framework for understanding, it is ultimately too abstract to help us to grasp important local meanings. Indeed, it is the local meaning of concepts that constantly defies our understanding. The local stamp of experience on emotions is tremendously important. If we think that our love is the same as Ifaluk love, and act accordingly in Ifaluk culture, it could get us into trouble, because the two loves carry different implications for social interaction.

When we name emotions we may feel that we are simply referring to what is naturally within all of us, a concrete entity called anger, for example. With this assumption in our unconscious mind we are apt to reason that they feel just like we do: every human knows what anger is regardless of its name, we might argue. But we have seen that this is only true in the general sense. This argument is another example of the fallacy of naive realism. That is, the belief that emotions are so basic to our species that we are all alike in this respect. The case of song suggests otherwise. Naive realism does not account for the power of local culture to mold the emotional norms of a group in dramatically different ways. Even within our own culture individuals sometimes find it difficult to empathize with another person's anger when shared experience is lacking.

Each culture values an *emotional style*: normative ideas about what kinds of emotions there are, when to express them, and with what intensity (Middleton 1989). As individuals growing up in a particular culture we learn an emotional style, part of which is usually governed by gender identity. In the United States, men are traditionally not supposed to cry except under certain unusual conditions; women are expected to cry more often. Emotional style is part of our identity and motivates us to act. A display or a statement of anger defines who you think you are both as an individual and as a member of a group. Ilongot men who hunt heads because of their grief and anger are making both individual and group statements (Rosaldo 1989:3).

Culture

Naive realism underestimates the degree to which learning a culture defines the borders of our lives. To recognize our naivete is to peel back another layer of our own culture, the inner layers of which are home to our deeply implicit, unconsciously held, culturally shaped assumptions about the way the world works. These assumptions, values, and ideas may rest concealed and undisturbed until challenged by an alternative reality. Even at the point of challenge we may not know the source of our uneasiness. Alverson was fortunate that her hosts were willing to speak so freely with her about their own assumptions regarding hospitality and serving kadi, in contrast to Fernea's experience in Marrakech where she never discovered why she was told to ignore the injured man in the street.

Culture is *learned* behavior; nearly all of human behavior is learned, excepting of course basic biological functions. The roots of the term culture are in French and Latin with connotations of nurturing and growing. Learning is a process of growing that needs nurturing. We learn ways of thinking, feeling, and seeing; we learn morals and meaning, and the practical arts of everyday life. While we do respond to the press of biological drives (for example, hunger and thirst), our responses are culturally guided. We can learn to control pain as do ritual fire walkers, yogis, and dancers of the Sun Dance (Williams 1983:161–71). The detailed cultural acts of our lives are not guided by genetic programming to the degree experienced by other social creatures. This fact leaves us with great flexibility of behavior by which to cope with rapidly changing circumstances. In terms of evolution we are generalized creatures whose survival depends upon flexible behavior.

While we stress the important role of flexible behavior, we need at the same time to acknowledge that we obviously also inherit at least general capacities for behavior that undergird specific behavior. Language, culture, and emotions are examples of the interaction between inherited capacities and learned behavior. Precisely where we will find ultimately the proper balance between inheritance (nature), and learned behavior (nurture), remains to be discovered. In the early part of the century when anthropology was establishing itself largely on the basis of the concept of culture and its priority in explaining diverse ways of life, a hard distinction was often made between instinct and learned behavior. It was necessary to point out that cultural variation could not be accounted for by reference to instinct, because a particular set of instincts is characteristic of a species. In other words, if humans are one species, and therefore possess but one set of instincts, how could behavior vary cross-culturally?

Behavior that varies cross-culturally is, in the old way of thinking, evidence against the operation of instinct. Thus for almost every proposed instinct, anthropologists discovered exceptions in the actual practice of a specific group of people. An instinct for survival is negated by the widespread act of suicide for personal and cultural reasons. An instinctual incest taboo (although a nearly universal cultural value) is negated by actual practice in most societies. Instincts for aggression and territoriality have not been substantiated. So where are those instincts?

We know today that the crude dichotomy between instinct and learned behavior inaccurately reflects the complex reality that actually exists between genome and behavior (Konner 1982). Specialists in evolutionary psychology and sociobiology are currently working on this relationship, but we cannot properly deal with this complex issue here.

We can, on the other hand, state with a high degree of confidence that variations in human behavior are not attributable to differences in "race." As we saw earlier, race is not a biological reality. Geographical variations give rise to superficial differences in size, shape and color, and have nothing to do with social, moral, or intellectual capacity (Gould 1981; Molnar 1983). An infant from any group can be taken from one culture and placed in another and do perfectly well in the new culture, provided that he has an equal opportunity. In this sense, humans are completely interchangeable.

Human behavior is largely learned behavior, and it is learned only in the company of other humans. Because we are born immature social creatures, there is no other way of acquiring culture than in the presence of other humans. Just how critical this requirement of social learning is can be driven home by considering the negative case of children who are isolated from the nurturing presence of other humans. Children who have been locked away in closets, attics, and basements at an early age, depending on the timing and severity of their experience, do not speak, nor walk, nor have any conceptions of themselves aside from being a crude bundle of drives and reflexes. Lacking the power of language, they have no sense of self, or personhood. Without language they can learn little of their culture or of themselves. Depending on specific conditions, these children, when given remedial instruction, learn slowly and are intellectually always behind others of their chronological age.

Specific cultures are not biologically inherited and therefore must be *acquired* by each child by the process of *socialization*, or *cultural transmission*, from one generation to the next. By this process, both the continuity of a culture is preserved and the next generation of individuals is made culturally competent adults. The succeeding generation receives the hard-won experience and knowledge of preceding generations. Most native peoples, for example, can name and use hundreds of species of plants, animals, birds, and fish. This is survival knowledge accumulated over generations of experience and experimentation; it could not be duplicated in a single generation.

The combination of accumulated experience and flexible behavior enhances our chances of surviving challenging conditions. For this reason, culture is said to be *adaptive*. We learn a culture so well that much of our behavior subsequently becomes *habitual* and *unconscious*. Individually, we *internalize* culture, which means that we accept it for ourselves and commit to it emotionally and intellectually. When we internalize a culture, we do not easily give it up.

The routine satisfaction that we derive from our culture normally outweighs occasional dissatisfaction and makes it painful for us at times to change. The world our culture constructs for us is so familiar that it seems to be the "right" or "natural" way of life. Because of our comfort in tradition and frequent discomfort with change, our flexible behavior often becomes inflexible. All cultures seem to suffer at times from this tension between old and new. This does not mean that we all become robots incapable of change, only that routine can be comfortable.

Effective group life depends on learning a common culture, and *sharing* common understandings and expectations. One of the roles of socialization is to instill in children the accepted customs of the group. Although socialization is not a perfect process producing identical persons, it does well in coordinating individuality. Humans do vary individually in temperament and aptitude, and these characteristics interact with cultural values and norms. In the words of Wallace ([1961] 1970:23), socialization does not "replicate uniformity, but organizes diversity." We are individuals living in groups, not cultural clones.

In spite of the general effectiveness of socialization, culture is not shared perfectly. Culture is based on a sharing sufficient to work effectively as a group. Even in simply organized bands of forty to sixty individuals (sometimes called egalitarian societies) males and females do not share culture completely because of gender distinctions. Generational difference leads to incomplete sharing. Age and sex are, in fact, two universal features of human life that result in a differential sharing of culture. As we came to live in ever-larger and more-complex groups, greater internal differences developed which led to various forms of social differentiation. The different life chances, for example, of those in various social classes in this country have been well documented for decades (Sennett and Cobb 1973). Those in the lower social class are more likely to experience crime, disease, poor schooling, and contact with welfare agencies than those in the middle and upper classes.

Cultures are systems of meaning and symbols (Geertz 1973). As we shall see later, we attach meaning to acts, things, and nature. Body adornment, hair style, and body language all have meaning. Burning the American flag is a symbolic act. The flag is a symbol whose mainstream meaning is known to all, but contested by some. That is, to some it is a symbol of freedom, to others a symbol of oppression. Burning it is to some an unpatriotic act, to others an act of defiance. What the symbol means is arbitrary, not fixed.

Subcultures, customs and beliefs that overlap with but depart significantly from the mainstream culture, emerge in nations for various sociological and historical reasons. Class, ethnicity, and perceived race are common sources of differential socialization. Subculture formation is most often understood as partly self-generated and partly imposed by a dominant culture on the basis of difference. However, a subculture is not merely a collection of different customs and beliefs, nor is it an incompetent imitation of mainstream culture. It is organized, systematic, and does not seek to imitate. Yet it remains with one foot in the pail of mainstream culture. These are important issues that we will revisit in the following chapter.

Language acquisition is a critical and integral part of socialization. Without it, we can not participate effectively in human life. Imagine the dark and lonely world of Helen Keller before she discovered language. The presence of language, and her eventual mastery of it, freed her from this dark world because she had gained the means of knowing herself and the world around her. She was able finally to establish nurturing relationships with others. A problem in either socialization or language acquisition usually affects the other because of this close interdependency, as Keller's case illustrates.

CHANNELING BEHAVIOR

Another way of looking at socialization is to see it as coordinating individual and group goals and means. Ideally, by the time a child reaches adulthood she has internalized the values, goals, and procedures accepted in her culture. Having internalized these mores, the person is able to be self-monitoring, acting in culturally consistent ways with little external prompting from others. In the process of learning her culture, the child also learns her identity and the roles she will be expected to play in life. Children are, in fact, generally taught what they need to know in order to be competent adults, as the cases of Temne and Inuit child-rearing practices substantiate.

Socialization and Social Identity

Socialization is a life-long passage and not limited simply to childhood. It is so important that most cultures in the world ritually mark the more important transitions in the life cycle. These rituals come under the general label of *rites of passage* (Van Gennep 1908). Life cycle events such as birth, transition to adulthood, marriage, and death are the most commonly recognized events. Human groups have a vested interest in channeling and marking life cycle events because they are particularly important to both the group and the individual. These events are foci of conflict and tension and therefore require an orderly handling to avoid unnecessary friction. They serve to define new statuses and to prescribe new rights and duties for the individuals entering a new stage.

The initiation rites common among native peoples usually involve prior instruction in the beliefs and morals of the group as well as the ceremony which marks the passage of adolescents into adulthood. In secular North America, formal education and graduation act much like rituals of passage, although some particular religious observances of transitions, such as confirmation and *bar mitzvah*, remain. Extending formal education into college and beyond blurs the change to adulthood (Moffatt 1989). Partly for this reason, the transition from adolescence to adulthood in mainstream American culture, compared to many other cultures, is poorly marked and delays recognition and responsibility as an adult.

Socialization turns raw humans into social persons, who then interact with each other on the basis of their social identities. Note that the Panare had trouble deciding who Dumont was, and therefore how to interact with him. On the other side, Dumont struggled with the question of how to present himself to the Panare. When Dumont became a "brother," his role-status-identity was established and his interaction with them better defined. Even in North America, with its stress on individuality, ambiguous identity, role, and status affect relationships

adversely. Such problems are particularly evident in cases of sociocultural change where roles and identities are being redefined. For example,
the feminist movement where women are seeking to redefine their traditional identity and to reassess their role in contemporary North American
life creates ambiguity at times for both women and men, with consequences for the quality of their interaction with each other.

Role, Status, and Self

A social system can be seen as an organization of roles and statuses.
A *role* refers to the behavior that a particular social person is expected to
display. A role entails certain rights and duties. Parents have both rights
over and responsibilities to children. A *status* is a recognized position in
the social system. Roles accompany statuses. It is useful to conceive of
roles as coming in pairs. Each role has a *complement*, for example, parent-
child, teacher-student, husband-wife. Complementarity can also be seen
working in that as women seek to redefine their identity and role in contemporary life, they necessarily call into question the traditional role and
identity of men as well.

The idea of role is drawn from the theater. A theatrical role is a
script that has already been written by the playwright and then played
or interpreted by actors. Each actor plays the role in a recognizable, but
individual way. No two actors will play a role in the same way. The same
is true in life. We are born into a world already made, roles already pre-
scribed, and we learn to fit into those roles. We will play many roles in our
lifetime, but none of us will play the same role exactly the way another
person will. The role of teacher is played competently by almost all qual-
ified individuals, but with considerable individual variation within
normal limits. Just because we fit generally into roles, however, does not
mean that we do so comfortably. Most of us, in all cultures, feel at least
occasional discomfort in established roles.

The concept of *self* is useful in making a distinction between role and
player (Erchak 1992). The self is a conscious, reflective, and interpreting
person. The self is the public person. The conscious self is aware of her
daily performance in roles, and the self monitors this performance constantly. Thus the self reflects on her activities and the responses of
others. The self interprets situations for their relevance to her own
actions, which the self may modify because of her interpretation. This
view underscores both the dynamic, process-oriented nature of the self
and the self-monitoring function of properly socialized individuals.
Acknowledging individual social awareness also balances the basic char-
acterization of humans as simply habitual, unconscious social actors,
which the internalized culture perspective seems to suggest. In addition,
it counters the popular misconception of "natives" as somnambulant
slaves to their customs. We all are both *habitual and conscious actors*.

Role definition has a political side to it. Who defines roles? Who defines identity? In a sense we all do because we approve and disapprove, reward and punish role performance. We all are agents of social control. Yet Native Americans, African-Americans, women, and other minorities are acutely aware of the fact that master roles tend to be defined by those who are in power (Carmichael and Hamilton 1967). They know that terms like "Indians," "Negroes," and "girls" identify them in negative ways that serve dominant power interests. These terms carry with them much biased and self-serving baggage, and their connotative meaning implies a lesser social status. Efforts to change negative public perceptions of minorities often include, but are certainly not limited to, changing negative labels that imply a stereotyped behavior. We will return to these issues later.

Anthropologists working in another culture cannot entirely avoid having to cope with the indigenous role system. The Ferneas, Obolers, and Alversons were learning this lesson as they settled into their host culture. The statement by Hoyt Alverson that they were becoming a Tswana couple is both accurate and revealing. In order to participate effectively, they had to adjust to existing expectations, at least to a minimally acceptable degree. By conforming to these expectations they learned more about the host culture than if they had chosen to go their own way. "Fitting-in" is part of the research strategy. Some cultures force the outsider to a strict conformity, but others permit more room for negotiation. Thus, if we declare our independence from the indigenous role system, we will lose much by doing so.

Morality

All cultures create value hierarchies. Morality refers to those values at the top of the hierarchy which are set aside and awarded additional importance. Morality implies emotional commitment, as well as the threat of punishment, to a set of values; otherwise the incentive to adhere to valued behavior would be weak. Commitment to morality creates an internal drive to the right behavior that is of obvious value in maintaining social cohesion.

Morality is integrated with the principal elements and issues of a culture. Among the Taita of Kenya, males are scrutinized through the years for their ability to construct a "moral career," and thus to achieve an honored elderhood. Most important in this career is their handling of anger, particularly in performing kutasa, an anger removal rite. The rite consists of making a declaration of anger and expelling fluid from the mouth, thus "casting out anger" (Harris 1978:138–40). The purpose of the rite is to cleanse the person, males most importantly, of the feeling of anger. It is both a personal and a social act. By executing kutasa, he makes his anger a public affair which involves others in solving the problem. In resolving the conflict, the community reasserts moral values, and reinforces group identity. If a male is known to harbor anger, but will not confess it through kutasa, he suffers a negative mark against his moral career, and against his very identity as a Taita male. In this single example, role, morality, gender and group identity, and the channeling of emotions are all demonstrated.

CONCLUSION

Humans evolved as one species sharing the same perceptual, cognitive, and emotional capacities. We survive on the basis of our ability to learn rapidly, to communicate complex ideas, and to transmit our knowledge to succeeding populations. Culture is learned behavior, constrained by inherited capacities which give general directions for specific and flexible behavior. Culture refers to values, ideas, expectations, things we make, clothing we wear, behavior we express. Culture shapes how we see things, what we make of what we see, and how we feel about it. We adapt to different environments and situations through culture. We survive with culture, perish without it.

Because individuals are born without detailed genetic programming for behavior, and because of our extended period of immaturity, we place a premium on learning during the socialization process. We learn our culture, and we learn who we are. We learn personal and group identity and prepare ourselves to assume roles as competent adults. These roles are culturally defined. We learn those morals and values that help us to define who we are and that guide our behavior along expected and appropriate channels.

All human groups possess a similar capacity to learn from experience and to create solutions to local challenges. All ways of life that exist or have existed constitute experiments in survival, but it is doubtful that any have failed because of the innate inferiority of a people. Diversity sprouts from common fertile ground. Raising boys and girls differently is a form of diversity, living in different cultures or different social classes are forms of diversity. Being physically or mentally challenged is a form of diversity. A complex organization of differentiated roles and experiences creates diversity. The borders of small worlds of experience are as vigorously defended as the borders of large ones. It is difficult for residents of the different worlds to communicate with each other across these borders. These experiential worlds, cross-cultural or intracultural, can be difficult to escape and equally difficult to enter, but continuing to skirmish only on their peripheries frustrates our discovery of common ground.

The key to unraveling human diversity, and crossing the borders of our own world, is to be found in probing the experience and interest of another group as filtered through those aspects of culture discussed in this chapter.

Chapter Three

Our Lived Difference

Simply being tolerant of diversity because it makes us feel good momentarily or because it is politically correct is a counterfeit tolerance. Without appropriate information and perspective, this stance leaves us poorly prepared to withstand ignorant but heated and biased assertions about other groups. It leaves us awash in the quickly and dangerously shifting currents so characteristic of issues in diversity. Arming ourselves instead with solid information, proven perspectives, and sharp analysis will better prepare us to handle the problem at hand. The problem we address in this chapter is to understand why and how diversity comes from our basic similarities.

Differences develop out of the fact that we live our lives in different places, different times, and different circumstances. We live in different neighborhoods of the world. We know our own neighborhood exceedingly well, but we know little of other neighborhoods. When, as distant observers, we see behavior in other neighborhoods that we do not understand, we try nevertheless to make sense of it. The act of interpreting and assigning meaning to seemingly diverse behavior draws from our experience in our own neighborhood, and that experience may be irrelevant to the one observed. Our interpretation is biased from the outset even though we do not intend it to be so.

We counter this local focus by extending the framework begun in the last chapter, where we established our commonality. We know that we must place behavior in its context, but now we can be more specific about how to do this. Three basic perspectives will help us: (1) culture as adaptation; (2) culture as meaning; and (3) culture as system. They are not the only perspectives that yield insights into the working of culture, but they will provide us with a satisfactory, if rudimentary, foundation upon which to build further insights.

CULTURE AS ADAPTATION

We have already defined culture as learned beliefs and behavior and noted that most of human behavior is learned within yet-to-be defined inherited limits. We further noted that we learn culture so well and so early in our lives that it becomes largely unconscious routine. Moreover, culture must be shared sufficiently well among members of a society to insure a minimal level of survival. Every day in countless ways we reproduce and reaffirm our culture by living it. Our daily behavior continues our culture, expresses it, and reinforces it. Culture accumulates over generations so that knowledge is not relearned each generation for the group as a whole, although, of course, children must learn their culture in order to become competent adults. Finally, culture is adaptive; we literally learn to survive in various localities and historical circumstances.

Whether finch, moth, or human, all species have adaptive characteristics that permit them to survive in their particular environments. The differing sizes and shapes of the beaks of finches in the Galapagos Islands impressed the observant Charles Darwin, and played a vital role in his formulation of the theory of evolution by means of natural selection. Variations in beak size and shape are adaptive—uniquely shaped to acquire particular food resources—to the many microenvironments in the Galapagos and on the mainland of South America where the finches are also found.

As the soot of the early industrial revolution darkened the trees in England, white moths were clearly visible to birds, their natural predators, and thus decreased in number, while dark moths were less visible and increased in number (Bishop, Cook, and Muggleton 1978). The change in the environment favored the survival of dark moths; their color was adaptive under changed conditions. These are biological adaptive mechanisms. Although we have described some of the superficial physical differences among humans as adaptive, in ancient times, to specific environments, we actually are able to live in a wide variety of environments today because of our ability to adapt through the use of culture. Culture is our adaptive mechanism. Our ability to learn quickly from experience and to mitigate the direct effect of the environment (clothing, shelter, fire, space shuttle) on our physical selves extends our range of adaptiveness to a wide variety of environments, some quite harsh.

By the time of our emergence in fully human form and function, at least 40,000 years ago, we had come to rely heavily on our unparalleled ability to learn the requisite survival skills to make it in quite hostile environments. Millennia ago we learned how to domesticate plants and animals, and this knowledge profoundly changed the human experience. We dramatically increased our food supply, settled down, and lived in larger settlements. Domestication occurred long before we discovered scientific methods, or the science of genetics. We learned instead by the pan-human processes of trial-and-error and observation, and by transmitting our accumulating knowledge over the generations. These are our survival skills.

Human adaptation almost always must include adjustment to the social environment as well as the natural environment, that is, to the presence of other groups of humans. We therefore developed the arts of war and diplomacy as well as food production, and these arts inform much of human history.

The idea of cultural adaptation has both positive and negative aspects. On the negative side, we cannot explain all human behavior as adaptive because successful adaptations of culture as a whole include behavior which might be in fact maladaptive, or even irrelevant. No group, for example, eats everything possible in its environment; beliefs and values may rule out certain varieties of edible plants and animals. Some seemingly useless practices continue because they are connected to other practices that are more central and adaptive. Other practices might continue for reasons of valued traditions rather than for any survival value. Survival is not usually threatened in these cases.

On the positive side, cultural adaptation requires us to look at a culture in terms of a people's perceived needs and real-life problems. The *adaptive focus* of a culture organizes a wide range of behavior and values toward achieving survival goals as we shall see in a moment. In this view, behavior has purpose instead of seeming to be a chance accumulation of isolated, aimless, and exotic actions persisting out of ignorance and tradition.

Early humans were nomadic, wandering from place to place as they foraged for seasonal food or searched for game. As we spread throughout the world from Africa to Europe and Asia, to Australia by 40,000 years ago, and to North America by perhaps 30,000 years ago, we were challenged by new environments. Like different languages branching and rebranching from a common linguistic trunk, cultures began to branch into different traditions. The archaeological record shows clearly that we were becoming more efficient and specialized as a result of occupying successfully a variety of habitats. Humans were perfecting arts of survival. With the domestication of plants and animals some ten thousand years ago, the nomadic life was abandoned by some groups as they remained sedentary to tend crops and herds. By this time the cultural tree was richly branched; diversity was well developed as different customs, beliefs, and values accompanied technological change in different environments. The common ground was already difficult to find.

Our main problem is to try to understand behavior that we at first do not understand by placing that behavior squarely in the context of real-life problems facing a certain group of people. Doing so undermines our tendency to make ethnocentric judgments, helps us to understand choices and constraints, and humanizes other people. In short, we need to understand the adaptive focus. Toward this end we examine several urban groups living in the context of poverty, but making somewhat different adaptations.

Poverty: African-American Inner Cities, 1960s

We are interested in studies of poverty in the 1960s for several reasons. It was a time in which first-hand studies of people in poverty began. These studies used the adaptational approach to show how people met a defined set of challenges, thus making their behavior more understandable to outsiders who tend to stereotype the poor as lazy, immoral, and incompetent. Indeed, the problem of poverty has not left us, and some of the same stereotypes and misconceptions of the 1960s remain with us today.

The 1960s was a time of great social upheaval in the United States, a time of inner-city riots, burning ghettos, and racial protests. This stormy period was witnessed by a stunned and puzzled public who nevertheless began to ask questions about causes and solutions. Although the unrest was answered by rather specific solutions focused on restoring inner-city African-American families, the mainstream public clearly did not understand what living in poverty was like, and they held many misconceptions and moralistic attitudes about behavior in the slums, regardless of race and ethnicity.

Academic knowledge of poverty was at this time based on second-hand social statistics gathered from census data, social service agencies, and courts and police—an information-gathering tradition which Charles Valentine (1968:22) exposed as grossly inadequate. With reference to one such work, he observes, "The reader does not get the feeling that the author has observed the life of slum dwellers intensively at first hand much less participated in that life" (p. 23). Data collected for administrative, rather than scientific, reasons were interpreted by those who had no intensive and prolonged experience in the context in which the data were collected. As Valentine feared, this tradition found its way into ultimately misdirected federal policies, largely in the form of the Great Society program of the Johnson administration.

A second line of thought emerging in the 1960s had at least the value of being based on first-hand observation and participation. The "culture of poverty" described people in poverty living an isolated, self-perpetuating life of violence, crime, alcoholism, and immediate gratification among other behaviors considered deviant. This idea was elaborated by Oscar Lewis in his work with Mexican and Puerto Rican families (1959, 1961, 1966). The "culture of poverty" is conceived as a subculture that exists in any class-stratified, capitalist society, and therefore not unique to the United States. The ultimate cause is the larger national and international economic and political constraints which actually set in motion the culture of poverty itself. The immediate cause of the behavior of poor people is a lifestyle featuring short-term adaptations to scarcity handed down over the generations, "the culture of poverty." Once this cycle settles in, it generates its own momentum that is hard to stop.

Many (Hannerz 1969; Leacock 1971; Valentine 1968) have noted the conceptual and theoretical inconsistencies in Lewis' work. (Unlike those before him, Lewis at least had first-hand contact with the people about whom he wrote). What most interests us here, however, is not general theoretical discussion, but how specific studies done in that era helped us to understand behavior as adaptive to poverty.

Eliot Liebow (1967) studied a small group of street-corner men in Washington, D.C., in the early 1960s. Although he focused on their street-corner activity he came to know them well and to know their social networks. He was particularly interested in their work experience. In one simple, but highly effective passage, Liebow describes a scene which an outsider would find difficult to interpret accurately.

> A pickup truck drives slowly down the street. The truck stops abreast of a man sitting on a cast-iron porch and the white driver calls out, asking if the man wants a day's work. The man shakes his head and the truck moves on up the block, stopping again whenever idling men come within calling distance of the driver. At the Carry-out corner, five men debate the question briefly and shake their heads no to the truck. The truck turns the corner and repeats the same performance up the next street. In the distance, one can see one man, then another, climb into the back of the truck and sit down. In starts and stops, the truck finally disappears.
>
> What have we witnessed here? A labor scavenger rebuffed by his would-be prey? Lazy, irresponsible men turning down an honest day's pay for an honest day's work? Or a more complex phenomenon marking the intersection of economic forces, social values and individual states of mind and body? (Liebow 1967:29–30)

Our response after reading the description of the street-corner scene more than likely matches the truck driver's, which is that the men don't want to work. Liebow goes on and identifies the men and the fact that some have already worked all night cleaning places such as banks and office buildings; some will go to work in retail stores in another hour or so; some work Saturdays and take their day off during the week; one is going to the doctor; one must go to court, and so forth. Thus, the interpretation of this scene from the insider's view is quite different. They all happen to be out on the street corner talking because they are going or coming on business, or for some other identifiable, justifiable reason. Street talk is a regular part of their lives. Being on the street, apparently doing nothing, and apparently refusing work, gives them a high visibility and makes them prey to biased preconceptions.

On the other hand, the street-corner man knows that the jobs he obtains are low-valued jobs, how could he not? He learns to hold menial tasks in the same contempt as do employers and society at large and has no commitment to them. He knows he is expendable, and low pay guarantees his knowledge of this (p. 212). These men learn to fail each day, in the present, not as an adaptive response to a culture of poverty, but because success does not guarantee them a better job; the era of the 1960s yields them few real options. These men also fail at their marriages, often blaming their own inadequacies and unwillingness to adjust their behavior. They fail because they cannot economically support a family. They fail because they are trying to achieve many of the values and goals of mainstream culture, but lack the tools and means by which to accomplish their goal. When they fail they try to hide their failure by rationalizing away their wish for a mainstream life (p. 222). Father and son fail independently because of the present, not because failure is handed down through the generations in a cycle of poverty.

Hannerz's *Soulside* (1969) is more of a community study in that it describes a variety of lifestyles, including both mainstream and street-corner men, sex roles, and expressive behaviors in a community context. Hannerz also criticizes the idea of a "culture of poverty," although he too sees elements of it being difficult to dismiss entirely. Children do grow up learning some behavior that is at odds with mainstream culture, that is self-destructive or anti-social, but this is neither inevitable nor irreversible. All cultures and subcultures contain maladaptive and self-destructive behavior, for example, in the United States, consumerism which is ecologically irrational.

Hannerz (1969) describes people who save, people who spend on personal expressive style, intact families, broken families, and street-corner men. People often express mainstream values although they don't always live them and indulge sometimes in "ghetto-specific" behavior (pp. 37–38). This fact does not separate them necessarily from mainstreamers who also do not always act in a manner consistent with espoused values. Anthropologists have come to expect discrepancies in ideal culture and actual behavior. However, Hannerz cautions against building a trait list of behavior that is either ghetto-specific or mainstream because the two categories are ends of a "complex continuum." Particularly, he fears isolating these behaviors from each other and from the larger culture, because they are all relevant to each other and to situations. Both types of behaviors are found in the same person and the same families at different times. Like Liebow, Hannerz underscores the economic weakness of the men as a major problem in maintaining mainstream lifestyles (pp. 74–75).

In another first-hand study of families in poverty in a midwestern city, Carol Stack (1974) argues against the assumption that female-headed families and illegitimacy are necessarily symptoms of "disorganized" families or broken homes (p. 44). She sees adaptation to poverty being based on the sharing—"what goes around comes around"—of scarce resources. Families share whenever they can; they cannot afford to ignore their reciprocal obligations to others, especially relatives, because if they do they become socially isolated. Loss of social support further jeopardizes their survival. In a support network, children may be raised by aunts or grandparents according to the distribution of resources in a network at any given time. In the eyes of the residents, whoever takes moral responsibility for raising a child is the true parent regardless of the biological relationship.

Support is where you find it, and it is not ascribed in formal terms of kinship or status. The family may be broken, but the support system is intact, giving the child an ordered and nurtured life. In this setting, the traditional nuclear family is but one part of a larger network of relatives and friends who contribute to the mutual support of all who are members in good standing. Outsiders such as welfare workers, by fixing on a traditional mainstream conception of a nuclear family, might then miss the importance of the support network.

Finally, Stack suggests that social welfare laws and policies are really intended to keep people on welfare, to prevent them from building equity and savings to become independent. The penalties incurred by welfare recipients for making too much or saving too much are disincentives for building any capital. When it is understood that initiative is not rewarded, mainstream preconceived and judgmental attitudes about social welfare participants being lazy are dispelled.

All three authors provided the reader with extended commentary on the conditions of their fieldwork, and their methodology. All exposed some popular myths about work, failure, and families in inner cities, and all connected inner cities empirically and conceptually to mainstream culture. They gave us additional insights into the full complexity of poverty and suggested different interpretations of observed behavior.

Poverty: Urban Italy

From another time and another culture, Thomas Belmonte writes a vivid description of adaptation to poverty made by poor families in the slums of Naples, Italy. Belmonte (1989:104) depicts life there as centered on what he calls the "triumvirate of want," love, food, and money.

These are the goals, in the context of poverty and violence, that generate the behavior and values of the residents; these goals define their adaptive focus. Children are treated with a mixture of love and violence so that they do not grow up too soft, or too trusting. People practice impression management in order to conceal motives and to protect fragile egos. Individual survival requires maneuvering for emotional advantage and the use of physical brutality.

Most households rely on a variety of income sources, both legal and illegal. Those who bring in cash on a regular basis remain integral members, but those who are older and fail to meet this expectation are in jeopardy of being asked to leave. We do not see in Naples the social support system noted by Stack. Households are more atomistic, more self-contained, and not so dependent upon a network of relatives and close friends.

The Neapolitan poor crave money because they don't have it, not because they want to display wealth as do the middle and upper classes. The money is for the present, for survival (Belmonte 1989:104). While this may seem obvious when stated, some of its ramifications for understanding observed behavior are not necessarily appreciated until seen from the inside.

> Being broke is an intolerable condition, analogous to sensory deprivation. It makes a man turn away from his children. It cuts him off from the good company of his friends. He cannot give, and is ashamed to take what is offered. Should he take then what is not offered? The inability to buy a caffe for oneself or to offer it to someone else can set a fire of bitterness growing within a man forcing him to choices and decisions which may alter irrevocably his image of himself and the world. (Belmonte 1989:104)

The personal costs to the individual are high as poverty weighs heavily on his relationships because of his mistrust and conflicted identity.

One area where he can exercise some control in his life is impression management, including the display of emotions and personal style of dress. Here he stage manages his public self for protection and interpersonal maneuvering.

> Perhaps this was why style was so important with the young men of Fontana del Re. For all their swagger, they yearned for acceptance by a society which had given them the snub. Style was something which they could appropriate and elaborate upon. Unlike literacy and salable skills, it was a manipulative part of social identity. Indeed, many of them risk imprisonment to dress well, not to eat. (Belmonte 1989:132)

Outsiders often misunderstand the reason for style expression, suggesting that if people are that poor they should not be spending their money on such frivolous things as fancy clothes. However, not spending on style does not mean that they have money to save; it would be spent alternatively on food, although they often go without meals in order to purchase "frivolous" things. Individuals need also to feed some basic psychological needs. Rather than being a failure of character in the face of hardship, style choice reinforces a fragile young identity against a brutal world. It is another less obvious ramification of the craving for money.

When Belmonte returned to the neighborhood years later, he visited the family that he knew so well. He happened to say to one of the children that the child could grow up to be a physician, but the family was unhappy with Belmonte because he had suggested to the child an unrealistic goal (1989:134). His suggestion blurred their adaptive focus.

Belmonte (1989:141) sees examples of Lewis' list of poverty traits in Naples, but notes that the people certainly know how to delay gratification; it is after all a constant feature of their lives. They purchase in bulk against future scarcity; they know very well that scarcity will visit them again. Yet when they eat, they eat well because they don't know when they will eat again. And while they sometimes do a number of other things that middle-class people do, they cannot *usually* do those things. Moreover, Belmonte argues that much of the behavior that matches Lewis' list is derived from the simple facts of unemployment and underemployment.

Poverty: The Santa Clara Canning Industry

A case study of the canning industry in Santa Clara, California, gives us an extended and contrasting example of adaptation to poverty while at the same time looking forward to discussions of culture as meaning and system.

After World War II, the Mexican-American population in Santa Clara jumped from 35,306 in 1950 to 226,611 in 1970 (Zavella 1987:49), partly because *Chicana* women quit their migrant labor jobs and moved to the city to work in the canneries. The major attraction was that working three to six months a year in the canneries (compared with working the whole year in the fields) could increase their household income for the year by between one-third and one-half. This allowed the family to abandon the migrant labor routes and remain in permanent residence. The women could also spend six months or more as traditional housewives, a role many valued. Even when working, they had a good opportunity to adjust shifts to complement their husbands' work schedule, and such arrangements reduced their need in the early stages of the family cycle to find babysitters.

Patricia Zavella (1987) studied Chicana women in their dual roles of traditional housewives and cannery workers. She sees her study as balancing the general view to be presented later in this chapter that economic expansion and increased employment opportunity necessarily open up avenues of job mobility for North American women. Zavella argues "that the structural constraints on women's lives and the ideology of family reinforce Chicana subordination. Within this context, women construct varied meanings of work and family." (1987:131). By structural constraints she means historical and economic setting, labor union competition for representation in the canneries, and the organization of work at the factories. The cannery labor market passed from craft production to factory system by 1937, through expansion and mechanization by 1968, and reached new levels of production and sophistication by 1978, whereafter it fell into decline. During the middle period, the teamsters won representation and the labor market segregated into a primary force for men and a secondary force for women. The early mechanization of men's work led to a job hierarchy, promotion ladder, and hourly wages, while women's work remained ladderless at piece-rates (pay per finished piece) even if their job happened to be mechanized.

The constraints of the work structure and the labor market were not the only problems the women encountered. The traditional conception of the family is that men work and support families and women take care of home and children. Men's wages are usually higher than women's. Yet men are employed in low-paying jobs that are often unstable, thus undermining the basis for the ideal family. Consequently, women often must find some way to secure additional income. At first, husbands see a working wife as a negative statement about their ability to support their family, and as having gained power in the domestic sphere. Later, husbands may change their minds as they become accustomed to the extra income. Women also gain some personal satisfaction, some independence, and enjoy camaraderie with other women in the workplace.

The decision to work usually was made in a discussion with the husband, who usually resisted at first and then "gave in" after the wife went to work. Later, husband and wife negotiated additional understandings. Men were concerned about their personal needs not being adequately served, and both husband and wife were concerned about household operation and child care.

In the later stages of the domestic cycle, with children on their own, women's income became more discretionary and was used for home improvements, new appliances, vacations, or college education for children. A number of families bought rental properties as a form of capital investment. Women continued to enjoy a camaraderie with other women at work which did not interfere with home and family so that home and work remained segregated from each other.

The women attempted to give meaning to their work by developing a work culture. "Workers use work culture to guide and interpret social relations on the job" (Zavella 1987:100). But they also had to develop the meaning of their work in the context of the traditional family, adjusting the patriarchal ideology of tradition. "The meaning women ascribed to their situation as working mothers included acceptance of their primary responsibilities as housekeepers and the need to adapt to the disruption of work" (Zavella 1987:133). The traditional ideology thus became more flexible in the eyes of men and women. Later, when there was less need for income, women still employed the ideology of the traditional family to justify the more personal desires to work. These two meaning contexts contrast with each other but obviously also complement each other.

From the Chicanas' point of view, their adaptation to poverty was the best solution for them at the time. But there was a cost to their decision to complement their family responsibilities, because part-time work reinforced their segregation at work and restricted their job mobility (Zavella 1987:98). On the other hand, they did not have many options, and any job they took would have been a dead end. Almost every form of cultural adaptation is imperfect, requiring trade-offs among several factors important to the participant. In this case they were "optimizing" their adaptation; they made the best decision for them given the variables important to them.

The number of canneries in Santa Clara fell from a high of fifty-eight in 1930 to eleven in 1982, replaced increasingly by electronics firms. Of Zavellas' original twenty-four informants, only five were still employed in canneries at the time of her writing. Most had retired. High wages and a shrinking market as U.S. consumers shifted to fresh fruits and vegetables sealed the fate of most of the industry.

The Santa Clara canning industry moved generally in tandem with North American industry, as part of a larger historical stream of industrial maturation and decline, where workers were replaced by high-tech equipment. Mexican-Americans, of course, had no control over these events, were poorly prepared for change, and thus could only adapt as they saw best.

No one could read this case study and believe that these women and men are lazy, lack intelligence, are driven by rigid tradition, or fail to use their income effectively—all stereotyped behaviors often erroneously attributed to the poor and minorities. If some Mexican-Americans are working in canneries, and if some are working as migrant laborers and others at other jobs, what do these different adaptations tell us about minority stereotyping? Joan Moore observes:

... that the American-Mexican population probably is more diverse in social composition than any immigrant minority in American history.

Therefore, no minority group less deserves simple stereotyping. ... (1976:1)

Moore demonstrated, over a quarter-century ago, the developing internal diversities among Mexican immigrants as they adapt to different historical, political, and economic circumstances in each of the border states where they live in large numbers. Indeed, the umbrella term, Hispanic-American, conceals as well the different experiences of Mexican-Americans, Cubans, and Puerto Ricans.

The notion of adaptation forces us to see behavior in its context, and from the viewpoint of the insiders. It helps us to see cultures and subcultures in dynamic relationships to the constraints and opportunities in their natural and social environment. This approach can be applied both to other cultures and to intracultural variation, such as perceived race, class, gender, and ethnicity.

CULTURE AS MEANING

The practical arts of surviving and striving are always accompanied by beliefs and values regarding their worth and their place in the world. In the words of Dorothy Lee:

The breaking of soil in the agricultural process may be an act of violence, of personal aggression, of mastery, of exploitation, or self-fulfillment; or it may be an act of worship, and the earth an altar. ([1959] 1987:1–2)

The widespread practice of farming is given local meaning. The meaning given is related to the historical traditions of the group and the larger cultural system in which it exists. One might, of course, argue that the essential meaning is clear: we need food to survive, but humans are never satisfied with such a utilitarian explanation, as Lee ([1959] 1987) notes, unless starvation is imminent. We are driven by our very nature to find meaning in our lives. To assign meaning to acts and events is to interpret them, to discover their relevance and therefore their consequences for us. To find meaning prompts us to form an attitude toward acts and events. Chicana women did not just work, they had to create for themselves the meaning of their work and their departure from tradition. Street-corner men knew the meaning of their menial work, and they knew its meaning in their lives, although they attempted to deny it. Style choice meant something different to young men in a ghetto of Naples than it did to outsiders.

Specific meanings are characteristically bundled into larger systems of meaning as part of a group's general emotional and intellectual outlook on the world around them. We are interested particularly in the social, the public and shared, aspects of meaning, not in personal meanings which would take us into the realm of individual psychology.

Meaning: Sensory Experience

The peoples who anthropologists study, including ghetto residents, often invite us to learn how to see, how to think, and even how to hear their way (Stoller 1989:121). In his *The Taste of Ethnographic Things*, Paul Stoller notes:

> This fundamental rule in epistemological humility taught me that taste, smell, and hearing are often more important for the Songhay than sight, the privileged sense of the West. In Songhay one can taste kinship, smell witches, and hear ancestors. (1989:5)

To understand how the Songhay of Niger (Africa) organize and give meaning to sensory experience, Stoller also had to appreciate how the senses have been handled historically in the West, the basis for his own meaning system. The key to sensory meaning in the West stems from the rise of Western science which is based on visual observation. Thus, seeing, rather than smelling, hearing, or touching, has emerged as the most important sensory experience. We peer through microscopes, read various scientific instruments, and observe subjects. His complaint about most scientific ethnography is that it may be too abstract and too far removed from actual experience, missing therefore the other sensory realities of daily life. Stoller wishes to peel back one more layer of ethnocentrism by inquiring into Western handling of sensory experience through a knowledge of other traditions.

Stoller is able to show how the Songhay's speech about their sensory experience is inextricably linked with social relationships. Sight, sound, and taste are organized by Songhay so that everything, from sauces to space, from name-praising to drumming, is given shared meaning. Sauces are good, bad, tasty, or bland according to situations and social relationships. They tend to be prepared best when Europeans visit (1989:16), although the staples are the same. When angry, or upset, a bad sauce will get across the point. Stoller and his associate were served a meal with an excellent sauce. The cook returned later clearly wanting to receive something from Stoller. At the next meal, he and his associate received a truly tasteless sauce because the cook was not happy with a black shawl his associate had purchased for her (1989:18–22). The same treatment could be extended to relatives—the quality of sauce being dependent on the current state of a relationship.

In his study of sounds as symbols in a Kaluli system of meaning, Steven Feld (1982), an ethnographer and jazz musician, focuses on songs, poetry, and natural sounds in the environment—especially birds—as these relate to Kaluli (Papua, New Guinea) culture. These sounds are conceived by the Kaluli as important parts of their emotional style and their social structure; meaning is merged with emotions and social relationships.

> As I wandered among the Kaluli, I began to find a pattern that con-
> nected myths, birds, weeping, poetics, song, sadness, death dance,
> waterfalls, taboos, sorrow, maleness and femaleness, children,
> food, sharing, obligation, performance and evocation. As I contin-
> ued to work through the materials, the pattern kept pointing to
> linkages between sounds, both human and natural, and senti-
> ments, social ethos and emotion. (Feld 1982:14)

The key to understanding connections among those elements mentioned by Feld is the central myth of becoming a bird, the key metaphor for all of Kaluli aesthetics. The Kaluli categorize birds in terms of their physical appearance and the type of sound that they emit. The use of songful weep-ing by women at funerals is considered to be the closest to being a bird, hence a gender variable is introduced. The act of keening relates grief to the myth of the boy who became a bird. As Feld puts it: "weeping moves women to song, and song moves men to tears" (1982:17).

The Kaluli talk about birds in many ways. They use poetic devices to involve audiences and to make them weep. Poetry is thought by the Kaluli to be "bird sound words" (Feld 1982:133). The Kaluli use nature and poetry to speak about their own experience in an emotionally power-ful and integrative way. The symbolic merging of nature and culture in native systems of meaning is an integral part of adaptation among indig-enous peoples.

The Kaluli and Songhay examples represent what Hanson (1975:17) calls *implicational meaning*.

> Every cultural thing, like the Rapan prohibition against drinking
> cold water when hot and perspiring, is linked by implication to oth-
> er cultural things, like a general hot-cold theory of health and dis-
> ease, and therein lies its meaning. (Hanson 1975:10)

He sees culture as a logical system, a patterned whole consisting of inte-gral parts. Avoiding a cold drink is linked to a system of beliefs about illness, its causes and cures. So some meaning derives from other, asso-ciated meanings, as a part of a coherent system.

The Kaluli know nothing about implicational meaning, which is a social science concept, a meaning assigned to insider behavior by outsid-ers. They simply do what they do for reasons that are good and sufficient for them. People are not concerned with whether or not they are acting adaptively, meaningfully, or systemically, which, again, are the descriptive and explanatory inventions of social science. The Kaluli are but one case among many in a strategy of cross-cultural comparison based in part on these concepts. The scientific meaning of acts and beliefs, which is likely part of a Western observer's background, thus overlays local meaning, hopefully without doing violence to its integrity. Any successful ethnography represents a balancing act between building comparative knowledge and accurately reporting the local case.

Intracultural Meanings

The subject of meaning has a political side to it. The meaning of poverty is not the same for mainstream North Americans and poor people. The meaning of race or gender is different for different groups. Mainstream North Americans will see the American flag as a symbol of freedom and opportunity, while some minority groups may see it as a symbol of oppression. Mainstream North Americans and Native North Americans interpret differently Columbus' "discovery" of the New World. Like other aspects of culture, meaning does not exist in a vacuum, but is firmly located in specific historical contexts—sensitive to the influence of power and wealth.

CULTURE AS SYSTEM

It is important to view behavior as part of a system. Most individual behavior is an expression of a cultural system of beliefs and norms, individuals acting as social persons. Individuals enact, however imperfectly, culturally defined roles and statuses. Roles and statuses are parts of institutions. Economic, political, family, and religious institutions are all part of a larger system. Textbooks in social science treat them individually in separate chapters, but this is a pedagogical strategy, not an accurate reflection of reality because in reality, they overlap. As institutions and practices are part of a cultural system, cultures themselves are parts of a larger system, at both national and international levels. All levels and system components are subject to historical influences. The essence of systems is the interrelationships among their component parts so that a change in one produces changes in other parts. Constructing the interstate highway system generated profound changes in North American life beyond the simple convenience of efficient travel by dictating shopping patterns, encouraging suburban growth, and undermining public transportation.

Cultural systems, however, are imperfect systems containing contradictions and inconsistencies, and usually undergoing some change.

They are sufficiently efficient, but not perfectly efficient. We might regard different systems as natural experiments, with some being more successful than others. Some flourish under change, some disintegrate, some manage to adjust enough to continue. Most sociocultural systems experience more change in some of their institutions than in others. Some parts might lag behind or even resist change.

The adaptational view stresses *external* relationships, while the systems view stresses the *internal* organization of culture. In stressing the internal aspects of a culture, we run the risk of isolating it from its context. It is easy to see that both views are needed. All cultures today are enmeshed in a web of worldwide relationships, internesting cultural domains, of which they are parts. Cultural systems then are not isolated, and therefore they are affected by changing contexts and outside influences, which is what makes them so interesting. Cultural systems are *open systems*.

Oscar Lewis thought that he saw a continuing set of relationships among certain behaviors that was a response to the conditions of poverty. He saw poverty as a closed subsystem or subculture which, while set in motion by larger historical circumstances, persisted on its own—the culture of poverty. He was not entirely correct, nor was he entirely wrong. What he did see correctly was a set of related behaviors that might be adaptive in the short run yet maladaptive in the long run, but he failed to stress sufficiently the fact that the culture of poverty, to the extent that it exists, is an open system. In other words, it is susceptible to ongoing, contemporary economic and political pressures. There is no inevitable, learned cycle of failure. Rather, the persistence of certain behavior is better explained by contemporary social and economic forces that envelope it. The following case studies illustrate interrelationships among different systems levels.

Gender Roles

We will introduce a number of system variables influencing gender definition and gender stratification: (1) the economy and labor market; (2) modes of food production influencing rules of residence and descent; (3) warfare favoring patrilocality; (4) relative income contribution between males and females; (5) degree of segregation between public and domestic spheres; and (6) level of sociocultural complexity.

Gender role definition, and consequently gender stratification, is sensitive to changes in cultural systems. Degree of sociocultural complexity is one important variable in gender definition. In hunter-gatherer groups—small, nomadic bands—the relationship between men and women is basically egalitarian (although not completely). Indeed, Draper (1975) shows gender roles to be interdependent and exchangeable among the traditional !Kung Bushmen. This finding is not surprising for a small face-to-face group where men and women are not heavily burdened with work. But when some !Kung became sedentary, gender separation developed more strongly as men travelled more and worked more away from home in search of cash.

Sanday (1981) found that where men contributed significantly more income/food in hunter-gatherer groups, gender separation emerged. The same thing happened when women made either a great deal more or less than men. Where men and women contributed about the same, they remained on an equal basis. Thus, even at the hunter-gatherer level, gender stratification begins when incomes between men and women begin to diverge greatly in response to local socioeconomic conditions.

At the next level of population size and sociocultural complexity, ranked societies (horticulturalists and pastoralists who produce more food), ideas of biological descent, and rules of residence introduce still other variables. In patrilineal societies where descent is traced through the male line, men's public power and authority are supported by descent principles. Usually this type of descent includes the rule of patrilocal residence, where the married woman must move to the place of her husband. Removed from many of their kin, women have less support than they would have if they lived in their home community. In a matrilineal society, descent is traced through the female line, and there is an avunculocal residence rule where the man and woman upon marriage move to her eldest brother's place. She is still with kin who support a stronger role, although her eldest brother retains public power and authority. The woman is not elevated to a dominant role but does move closer to an equal partnership in many avunculocal descent groups.

Rules of residence and descent are influenced heavily by modes of food production. A change in the circumstances of food production can cause a change in these rules. In their effort to increase manioc flour production for rubber tappers in the Amazon Basin, the Mundurucu changed from patrilocal to matrilocal residence pattern so that mothers and sisters could work more productively.

Ranked societies are much more prone to warfare than hunter-gatherer groups, and thus men are more highly valued as warriors. Women, on the other hand, become more important as food producers. Gender stratification is very clear. Martin and Voorhies (1975) discovered that, in a sample of over 500 such societies, over 50 percent showed women doing most of the cultivating, while women and men cultivated about equal amounts of time in 33 percent. Men worked more in the fields in 17 percent of the sample.

Margolis (1984) documents shifts in attitudes toward women in the United States as the economy and labor needs of the nation changed. Attitudes toward working women relaxed, for example, during

World War II when women were required to enter the labor market in
great numbers as men were sent off to war. After the war, the attitudes
against women in the workforce began to harden again as men returned
from service looking for work. Industrial expansion after the war, however, did accommodate many women who wished to continue working as
well as new workers. Expansion of the economy provided an avenue for
women to make good on their political protests in contrast to the early
part of the century when opportunities to do so were severely limited.

Against this trend today is the large number of women in poverty,
or in transitional states on welfare, because of divorce, loss of husband,
or other factors. Also, women tend to be in lower paying jobs, and where
there are opportunities for advancement, there are often obstacles on
the rungs of the promotion ladder.

Attitudes and definitions often flow from changes occurring in a
system. When there are changes in role definitions, whether gender-
based or otherwise, people reflect on, or give meaning to, what is happening. Zavella's report on cannery workers serves as an example. On
the other hand, people can, as women have, directly address gender definition and stratification through political action. Remembering that a
society can be seen in terms of a role system, we can see that changes in
the definition of one role necessitates change in others. The husbands of
the Chicana cannery workers were challenged to rethink their own traditional role, regardless of whether they actually changed their
attitudes or behavior.

Ethnicity

Studies by Zavella and Moore cited earlier show us how Mexican
and Hispanic-American groups must adapt to different socioeconomic
contexts in the Southwest, West Coast, and other urban areas of the
United States. Cubans, who were particularly well educated, were well
received by the United States as they fled the Castro revolution in the
1960s. It should surprise us little that they have done so well. Other
Hispanic-American groups have had varying degrees of preparation,
opportunity, and success in other parts of the country. Although they
are often stereotyped as a uniform group with an "essential identity,"
that is, as having some sort of internal quality that marks them no matter what country or time they come from, what actually defines them
more sharply is their *relationship* to historical, social, and economic circumstances as suggested by the Cuban case.

In his *Ethnic Groups and Boundaries* (1969), Fredrik Barth notes
that ethnicity and ethnic identification are historically shaped and
stand in dynamic relationship to the encompassing social system.
According to Barth, we should shift our attention from specific tradition
and particular beliefs—the internal stuff of ethnic identity, or an essen-

tialist definition—to external relationships. Rather than centering on culture content, we should ask what causes ethnicity to emerge (Barth 1969:17). This perspective allows us to see that ethnicity is more about power, wealth, and competition than it is about traditional ethnic essence. This point needs further illumination.

There is a great tendency to see groups of people in terms of their differences from us. They look different, act different, speak a different language. When they say and do things that we do not like, we attribute it to who they are—to the idea that they are different in an essential way. And while we cannot completely dismiss the influence tradition has on fostering differences, Barth is trying to get us to look past the simple fact of difference and instead focus on the relationships among groups as being more important to understanding ethnic group dynamics. Why is it, he would ask, that tensions between groups rise and fall while the cultural difference between them remains the same? That is, their ethnic essentialism has not changed. What has changed in most cases is their relationship to power, wealth, or territory and thus to each other. The fact of difference too easily and deceptively becomes the rationale for prejudice and discrimination and the cause of trouble. It causes us to look in the wrong place for sources of friction.

In times of economic hardship and competition, ethnicity is accentuated and the boundaries between groups hardened, while in good times with reduced competition boundaries are relaxed. If each group occupies a specific economic niche as often happened in our early history (one immigrant group dominates laundries and another restaurants), the situation might be different. As Barth (1969:27) notes, interdependence depends on complementarity not competition, on stability not change. In direct competition, on the other hand, one ethnic group might displace another, but both stand to lose something because of the potential hostility and conflict between them. For example, the violent acts of skinheads against immigrant laborers in Germany in the 1990s rose in response to the nation's merging of East Germany with West Germany, suddenly creating an excess labor market at a time of economic recession. The two groups perceived that they were in direct conflict with each other. In this context, the ethnicity of immigrants emerged as a salient issue for some Germans, and boundaries tightened. In Northern Ireland, religious difference is only a superficial difference (Darby 1976). The violence is not really over religious dogma, but over political and economic dominance and artificially drawn boundaries. The same is true in the former Yugoslavia, where ancient differences and misdeeds emerged when the Soviet Union departed, leaving a power vacuum. A troubled past is used by present leaders to justify violent acts (Butler 1992). Because they are used for present purposes, these past experiences are open to distortion, half-truths, and stereotyping in order to heighten emotions and to increase social solidarity within a group.

Barth's perspective furnishes us with a key by which to understand that ethnicity is not just a matter of cultural heritage, but a dynamic reality in the contemporary world. The content of an ethnic culture may remain the same through generations, but ethnic conflict occurs typically in the context of shorter term economic and political competition as shown above. Clearly, anger and violence can erupt out of simple ignorance and prejudice, but it is the use of perceived difference in a particular competitive context to justify acts against others that most interests social scientists.

Finally, ethnicity, social race, gender, and poverty are all embedded in power relationships which interfere with a more tough-minded, cultural relativist understanding of how difference is used. Power entails the ability to impose names, labels, identities, and values on others that bear consequences for them.

CONCLUSION

By examining the adaptative, systemic, and meaning facets of culture we build a suitable framework by which to understand diverse behavior, at least on a preliminary level. By specifying the real life challenges that a specific group of people face we make sense of their behavior, while preserving their humanity. Seeing different lifeways as related to other lifeways and larger social entities helps us to avoid isolating people from the forces that impinge upon them and influence their behavior. By inquiring into the meaning that people assign to their acts we derive a better appreciation for the human need to make sense of the world and our place in it. The examples presented in this chapter depict a "lived-in" world of challenges to which people must adapt. We are now prepared to examine in more detail some of the problems we can encounter in actually removing prejudice and misunderstanding from our view of the other.

Chapter Four

Mirrors and Chasms

When we look at others, we are looking at ourselves too. We see similarities and we see differences. Comparison is inevitable. We locate ourselves in the sea of human variation by comparing ourselves with others in order to know who we are, or who we are not. Clyde Kluckhohn observed:

> The scientist of human affairs needs to know as much about the eye that sees as object seen. Anthropology holds up a great mirror to man, and lets him look at himself in his infinite variety. (1960:16)

In this famous passage, Kluckhohn recognizes the comparison that is implicit in our observing others and suggests that we might gain more objectivity about ourselves through an understanding of the sheer variety of cultures that we encounter. In this way we more accurately locate ourselves in the wide range of human variation and achieve a fresh perspective of ourselves. Kluckhohn makes the case that it is easier for the anthropologist to view remote ways of life with detachment and "relative objectivity" (p. 17) because the scene is so different. Kluckhohn focuses on cultural difference.

Kluckhohn's mirror metaphor was useful in helping the public understand what anthropologists of that day were up to and how all people might benefit from their work. However, it does not hold up well in these more contentious times because the mirror is passive, it merely reflects. There is no guarantee that we will recognize the reflected image of ourselves as observers, and catch the fresh perspective. Today the "objects," or subjects, seen are not passive but more vocal about themselves and more critical of the observer than they were in Kluckhohn's day. They want to add to the mirror their own often strident voices, their own images. Active engagement of Westerners by others is now a fact of life, an attitude that social scientists are compelled to confront whether or not we wish to. We no longer have a choice. In the past we have too often engaged in a monologue among ourselves about ourselves through others, but now is the time for dialogue. Mirrors, voices, and the eye establish the key metaphors that inform this chapter as we examine our self-critical attempts to understand ourselves and the efforts of the observed to discover their own voices in the modern world.

COLONIALISM AND RACISM

Europeans were intellectually unprepared for the discovery of the New World where they found people who were not only unknown but were not supposed to be there in the first place, according to their view of the world. But they were intellectually prepared to accumulate trade goods, precious metals and gems upon which to build the modern European nation, according to the economic philosophy of *mercantilism*. European populations were small and spread thinly across the globe. Developing farms, mines, and other projects therefore had to draw substantial amounts of labor from indigenous peoples, most of whom had to be coerced into service by any number of techniques from outright slavery to a tax on their very existence, a "head tax," payable in cash only. Cash could be obtained only by entering the European economic system on its periphery. Native peoples did so at a severe disadvantage because of their lack of knowledge of the system, lack of resources, and paucity of marketable skills. They were nevertheless drawn inexorably into the unending search for cash.

In the context of conquest and colonization there arose a virulent, worldwide assault on the humanity and dignity of humans in the form of *systematic* racism. Prejudice and discrimination certainly existed in the world prior to slavery, and no doubt have been with us since antiquity. The Europeans expressed racist ideas even among themselves, although not on the basis of skin color, before slavery. The English brought with them to the New World particularly rigid (compared to Europe) ideas about race that grew out of a folk classification which contained the classic elements of ranked differences, inherited ability, and a close connection between outer characteristics and inner qualities (Smedley 1993). Indeed, they had such ideas about the Irish who they utilized in North America as indentured servants. Yet, racism in the context of slavery was a mutant form, new in its widespread and systematic connection to exploiting the labor of people and appropriating their land. As Smedley points out, the English had very intense feelings about property rights and individualism which made them protective of their enterprise in slavery, where humans are owned as property.

The technological superiority of the West reinforced its sense of moral and cultural superiority. Communities the world over, suffering from shock, devastated by diseases against which they had no resistance, entered a new culture that they did not understand under terms dictated by dominant Europeans and Americans. Many groups fled momentarily out of harm's way, while others mounted fierce, extended and frequently effective resistance.

By far the most devastating technique of control, because it continues to wreak group and personal damage in myriad ways, was the attack upon the psyche of the victims through racist ideas. Burkey (1978:95–101) offers a classification of racist ideas employed in controlling people during the initial contact and subsequent colonial periods, yet which are still with us in one form or another. These are ideal types, of course, and reality matches them imperfectly, but nonetheless they give an acceptable overview of racism.

Conflict racism sees subjugated people as treacherous savages, sinister foes, and cunning warriors. They are seen as dangerous and effective in the short run, but no match for advanced cultures in the long run. They lack the qualities of valor and intelligence, not to mention the technology to conduct superior offensive maneuvers. These attitudes were characteristic of many frontiers around the world.

Paternalistic racism is a condescending attitude among politically and economically dominant peoples who see native peoples as charming primitives, happy children, or pathological victims. This pattern of stereotypes persisted in North America until recently as portrayed, for example, in early U.S. movies. No better is the idea that subjugated peoples are more like domesticated animals. Burkey points out that modern liberals seized on social pathology—the results of being past victims of prejudice and discrimination—as a substitute for the idea of genetic racial inferiority. He notes Kenneth Clark's point in *Dark Ghetto* (1965) that contemporary social deprivation theories (that people living in the ghetto are not socialized properly for the mainstream because of discrimination) are much the same. But inhabitants of the ghetto are victims of the present as well as the past as we saw earlier in our discussion of urban poverty. Although racism existed before, it took on a particularly systematic and pernicious form with colonialism and is still with us in various guises.

Decline and Degeneration

The existing orthodoxies of Medieval and Renaissance Europe simply did not handle conceptually the existence of exotic peoples; Europeans' worldview, not surprisingly, covered mostly themselves. There were, however, collectors of exotic customs known as *encyclopedists* and *cosmographers* who were popular. One of the more famous of these is

John Boemus who wrote his *Fardle of Fashion* (1555) in which he tried to assemble the entire range of human customs, a true "cabinet of curios." Interpretations of the meaning of these curious customs were left to the reader.

These and similar works exoticized and, in modern terms, marginalized the humanity of newly discovered peoples. Differences were emphasized in comparison with European standards to the extent that perceptions of cultural differences raised questions about whether these people were human and part of the biblical story of creation. Because Europeans saw these exotic peoples as having been isolated from Christianity and civilization, they came increasingly to be seen as degenerate and therefore to be preyed upon or at least to receive the benefits of contact with the church and civilization.

> Patristic ethnology has divided the old world between the descendants of Shem, Ham, and Yaphet and thus made all men descendants of Adam, and participators in his sin and fall. The first view of the Spaniards, as soon as they knew that the Americans were a new race, was that they were outside the grace of God, and therefore their natural prey. In spite of the papal declaration of 1512 that the Amerindians were descended from Adam and Eve, the fact that the Pope had divided the world between Spain and Portugal and the desire for gold gave a crude justification to the appalling cruelty of Cortez (1519) in Mexico, and of Pizarro (1533) in Peru (Penniman [1935] 1965:35).

Decline and degeneration were ideas supported in the minds of adherents by such reported practices as cannibalism (the extent to which cannibalism was actually practiced is questionable), witchcraft, beliefs in ancestral spirits and strange systems of family and marriage. The doctrine of degeneration, materialistic greed, misinformation and misunderstanding, and the need for large pools of inexpensive labor justified the subjugation and cruel treatment of peoples and gave the world a viscious and tenacious complex of ideas that plagues us today.

THE NOBLE SAVAGE

The Europeans conducted a monologue among themselves about these new peoples in the sense that, while they were eager for new information, often fantastically distorted, from the reports of various travellers and explorers, they were not seriously interested in what the indigenous peoples had to say about themselves or about Europeans. Hence they did not enter into a productive dialogue with these people. Instead, various factions of Europeans discoursed with each other about the meaning of the customs and practices of indigenous peoples. Thus, against the doctrine of degeneration, which degraded exotic peoples and made Europeans feel better about themselves, European cultural critics used the image of naked innocence, cleanliness, sense of community, and lack of greed reported for many such peoples to critique moral decline in Europe. They created the image of the Noble Savage. While on the surface this idealistic notion would seem to restore dignity to native peoples, it, in fact, served mostly European interests. In France, those who had never been near Brazil used the accounts of Vespucci and others to call for revolutions and independence. Jean Jacques Rousseau, who based his model of the Noble Savage on the the Hottentots of southern Africa, but whose ideas of goodness came directly from Brazilian Indians (Hemming [1978] 1987:23), used these sources to advance his ideas about the current state of European political structures. Montaigne, the political theorist, created a dialogue in his *des Cannibales* (Hemming [1978] 1987:21) in which he had the Tupinamba (Brazil) questioning King Charles IX about the obvious injustices in France. He used the Tupinamba only as political foils. The Noble Savage distorts the truth as much as degeneration does by romanticizing native peoples to the other extreme.

The doctrine of decline and the idea of the Noble Savage demonstrate the fact that people try to make sense of differences and similarities in terms of their own preexisting cultural frameworks. Information about native peoples was molded to fit European ends. Few Enlightenment and Renaissance scholars were, in the end, really prepared to admit savages to the ranks of civilization, equal with themselves. The cultural mirror in this case was misused because they saw what they wanted to see. Native voices were heard, but not listened to.

INDIGENOUS RESPONSE AND RESISTANCE

Indigenous peoples were no more prepared intellectually than Europeans for the sudden arrival of equally exotic people. In general, the Indians of the Brazilian Coast received the explorers peacefully and with curiosity. They were, of course, fascinated with firearms and with how metal cut wood, but were not necessarily appreciative of strange European values.

The inhabitants of these faraway places also interpeted strange phenomena based upon their own experience and their own way of seeing things. The inhabitants of Highland New Guinea had never before seen the imprint of shoes with oddly patterned marks on their soles. These strange marks suggested to them the foot of a strange and perhaps frightening skeletal creature who had come from the wrong direction and walked across the country rather than using the established trails of the region (Schieffelin 1991:79). What kind of creature was this, they asked? What did it mean? On the other hand, members of the Hides expedition into the New Guinea highlands, whose footprints so puzzled the inhabitants, were amazed to observe valleys with farms laid in regular patches reminding them of English farms (p. 110). But how could something so familiar exist in such a primitive place, they wondered (Schieffelin 1991)? Something odd in a familiar place, something familiar in an odd place, both groups struggled to draw meaning from the new experience based on their past experience. Neither was equipped with the experience or intellectual framework to fully comprehend the shock of the new.

Initial contacts between visitors and hosts were often peaceful ones with exchanges of goods and curiosity about each other. The story of Native Americans tutoring early settlers on the East Coast in the arts of survival, including how to raise corn, are well known. And, although the explorers were after what they thought were more precious finds, the New World provided settlers eventually with much more valuable materials in the form of corn, cotton, tobacco, chocolate, coffee, potatoes, and sugar. These and other contributions of Indians are often forgotten (Weatherford 1991). Early peaceful relationships did not, however, usually persist.

A Tupinamba of Brazil noted to a French Jesuit:

> In the beginning the Portuguese did nothing but trade with us, without wishing to live here in any other way. At that time they freely slept with our daughters, which our women . . . considered a great honor. But the Europeans invariably began to insist that the Indians help them build settlements, and fortifications to dominate the surrounding country. And, after having worn out the slaves taken as prisoners of war, they wanted to take our children. (Rosenstiel 1983:27)

Eventually, most frontiers involved considerable violence on both parts as Europeans pushed on and native inhabitants defended their land. All over the world Europeans conducted wars of extermination against indigenous peoples. On their part, native peoples resisted, often scoring impressive, if temporary, victories. Plains Indians won a major victory against Custer in the United States in 1876, and the Zulu against the British in Africa in 1879 before being defeated by overwhelming firepower. Other peoples waged long and effective resistance wars against great odds. The Maori wars in New Zealand lasted for twelve years, and Maori courage and skill won the praise of the British troops (Bodley 1990:49).

There were many administrative techniques and ethnocentric justifications for bringing indigenous peoples into the European socioeconomic system. Slavery and the head tax mentioned earlier were the more crude varieties. Progress, education, and consumerism were three more powerful ways of enveloping such groups.

To Westerners, then and now, the idea of progress has a magical quality which justifies economic expansion and the culture of consumption, but hides not so obviously a multitude of sins. Indigines who refused, because of their pride in their own way of life, to enter the new system were said to be resisting progress, to be presenting irrational impediments to inevitable change. Cultural practices repugnant to Westerners, such as shamanism and polygyny, and traditional uses of land were obstructions to progress. Land not used for grazing cattle, Western styles of farming, or mining, was considered by the West to be nonproductive. Native peoples who did not appreciate this fundamental idea were thus refusing (or were unable to understand) to be assimilated into an obviously (in Western eyes) superior culture (Bodley 1990:97–98).

Education in missionary- and government-run schools undermined traditional authority and values, and supplanted them with the ways and views of Westerners. Education introduced a new language and new customs while usually denigrating traditional ways. It aimed at nothing less than the transformation of students to the point of assimilation into Western culture, albeit it in an unequal relationship. The lessons of a missionary or government education were more often those of respect, obedience, and politeness than those of fostering intellectual inquiry and an independent spirit (Bodley 1990:103–4). In North America, Indian children were sent to boarding school because it forced their permanent separation from the community (p. 104). The individual may lose self-esteem as he is buffeted by swirling currents of new and old ways. Education threatens to destroy a traditional sense of self and group membership. Such cultural discontinuities exacted a severe toll on native peoples. On the other hand, a common language could serve as a basis for pan-tribal unity.

Consumerism, based on the infinite expansion of markets for manufactured goods, was also an effective way of bringing "primitives" into the fold. A taste for clothing and technology insured the native quest for cash. An individual would have to enter the system on unequal terms because that was the only way to earn cash. As Bodley points out: "Forced labor, depopulation, reduced land base, loss of traditional food resources, and taxation all helped create a dependency on external goods" (1990:119). Add to these the concerted efforts of governments to introduce superior farming techniques and new or superior livestock, and to convert subsistence land to cash crop enterprises, and a considerable amount of change has already taken place. Education, religion, and consumerism complete the job of conversion to Western ways.

The gains made by Westerners in these faraway places were usually made at the expense of native populations, and instrumented by means of coercion, treaty reversals, and dubious land purchases. Much damage was accomplished by the courts and legislative bodies which legitimized the process of disenfranchisement. These techniques of control were justified by an underlying Western belief in its own superiority and its mission to civilize the remainder of the world.

IMAGES AND MYTHS

A very large part of understanding bias is to understand that when we appear to be talking about someone else, we are more often talking about ourselves, using the other to make important points, as did Montaigne and Rousseau. All peoples do the same thing as they interpret events in terms of their own experience and interests. Unfortunately, the historic power differential in favor of Westerners makes their colloquy more consequential for others. In this section, using examples drawn from photography, art, literature, and film, we examine how we perpetuate and disseminate images and myths about other people.

The Power of Images

In their critical study of *National Geographic* (1993), Lutz and Collins reproduce a photograph from a 1925 issue in which an African porter is pictured peering into a mirror held by a white woman in safari clothes who is laughing and looking at the camera. The caption accompanying the photograph reads "His first mirror: porter's boy seeing himself as others see him," with the authors' additional caption suggesting that this really means that self-awareness comes with Western contact and technology (p. 210). It is as if there is no other way to self-reflection. Mirrors reflect images, cameras capture them. They both intrude into the lives of others. Power adheres to those who make and dispense mirrors and to those who point the camera and keep the image. In the present example, the idea is that supposedly both camera and mirror evoked in the indigenous person a childish feeling of the miraculous (p. 211). At least, this is the Western imagination.

Photographs of native peoples with mirrors and cameras is a common theme in *National Geographic*, perhaps because for North Americans they are tools for self-awareness. Showing such photographs of them to North Americans resonates on two levels: they are so common in North American life and they play on stereotyping non-

Westerners as "childlike and cognitively immature" (Lutz and Collins 1993:207). A camera is both for observation and surveillance as well as for reflection (p. 207), facts which further complicate its use.

National Geographic's subscription rate is third behind *TV Guide* and *Reader's Digest*. But unlike them, it is the principal purveyor of images drawn from areas outside our border. Established in 1888, it soon became a common feature of middle-class households, which had "aspirations toward the educated, cultured life style of upper middle class professionals" (p. 17). *National Geographic* tries to adhere to humanistic principles and does not intentionally demean its subjects, which is precisely what makes it a good subject of study. It is not an academic journal, although its status on this score is ambiguous to many of its readers. It is in fact a highly successful commercial operation which depends more on not offending readers and giving them what they expect than challenging them. For example, countries out of political favor with the United States get less coverage—none on the former Soviet Union between 1945 and 1959 (although it may have been difficult for outsiders to gain entry) (p. 122). Latin America, particularly Mexico and Central America, received disproportionate coverage (p. 124–25). When China was reopened to the West, eight articles were published in the following ten years. According to their own surveys, *National Geographic*'s articles on Africa are the least popular, and those involving social problems in that area, least of all.

The Pacific is a popular region, and the photographs tend to feature women with bare breasts, often dancing. Men are shown as skillful navigators in traditional canoes. Another common theme is the arrival of the modern world, where, for example, one photo shows an Islander's navigator stick next to a radar screen for maximum contrast.

The Melanesian Islands, so named because the inhabitants are darker skinned than their neighbors, receive different treatment than other Pacific Islanders, with many photographs showing men peering into mirrors while applying facial paint and other decorations accompanied by captions suggesting pride and primping. These are images and words that draw contrasts between the viewer and those who are shown.

Women are frequently depicted as hard working, exotic, or beautiful objects, but primarily aspiring to be like Western women. Black women are treated differently. "The racial distribution of female nudity in the magazine conforms in pernicious ways, to Euroamerican myths about black women's sexuality, lack of modesty in dress places black women closest to nature" (Lutz and Collins 1993:172).

These photographs are not objective records, but instead they mirror for the viewer his own fantasies and unrecognized ignorance of other people, his ethnocentrism. They make the viewer feel better by meeting the viewer's expectations, rather than by challenging them. They do not encourage a reflexive attitude.

The Educated Eye

Primitive art offers a pointed example of how the West appropriates, categorizes, and judges aspects of other cultures. It illustrates how various Western interests converse among themselves about others, instead of with others. As Price puts it, the subject is ". . . those who have defined, developed, and defended the internationalization of Primitive Art, and on their racial, cultural, political, and economic visions" (1989:5).

This is not the place to explore various definitions of primitive art, except to note that we have the usual problems of trying to define an enormously diverse world of objects representing various technological capacities, styles, and interests, too conveniently wrapped in a highly questionable classification. The term obviously carries with it a heavy load of ethnocentric baggage. Our focus, instead, is as Price puts it: How the West has used that material covered by the term, primitive art.

The fact that Western self-appointed "experts" imagined more about the wellsprings of primitive art than they knew about the cultures and the artists themselves meant that they could give free rein to their own fantasies and ethnocentrism about the subject. Many connoisseurs seemed to think that they had a natural gift for knowing what was good, unsullied by their own culture. Somehow, whatever the provenance of an art object, they thought that they had a universally applicable taste for fine art. Price joins other anthropologists (Bourdieu 1984; Sahlins 1985) in noting that there is no eye that has not been educated (1989:19). The expert eye is still a product of its experience and culture and does not automatically perceive the designs and products of other cultures in unbiased light.

The West creates many myths about primitive artists. One is their childlike quality:

> Just as children cry when they are hungry and coo when they are content, Primitive Artists are imagined to express their feelings free from the intrusive overlay of learned behavior and conscious constraints that mold the work of the Civilized artist. And it is this quality that is most often cited as the catalyst for understanding between Westerners and Primitive artists. (Price 1989:32)

As she further notes, the racist foundation underlying the notion that primitive art is like children's art is rather transparent (p. 32). African art is particularly labelled in such fashion. Blacks are often thought to represent the childhood of humankind—stalled at an earlier stage of development. Again, we find that the dialogue is in one direction only.

> *We* partake of an identification with African art; this allows *our*
> self-recognition and personal rediscovery and permits a renewed
> contact with *our* deeper instincts; the result is that *we* increase *our*
> understanding of *ourselves* and *our* relationship to art. (Price
> 1989:37) [italics in orginal]

Price continues with the pithy comment that the Noble Savage and the
Pagan Cannibal are the same person "described by a distant Westerner
in two different frames of mind" (p. 37). It is not the case, of course, that
we should refrain from trying to make sense of primitive art in terms we
can relate to our own world—translating culture as we translate languages—but that we should understand our forms of self-deception.

A series of self-deceptions and misunderstandings mark Western
discourse on primitive art. Primitive artists are often characterized as
slaves to tradition, fears, spirits, and eroticism because they are close to
nature, or undeveloped. It is therefore reasoned that they are probably
not making conscious design choices based on clearly articulated aes-
thetic principles. We tend to locate them in a timeless past, rather than
in their struggles with the modern world. Contrasting modern art and
primitive art places cultural distance between them and us (p. 63).
These beliefs reveal a widespread ignorance of other cultures and dehu-
manize others as unreflective and unchanging people.

Another critical ingredient in maintaining distance is the fundamental difference in the amount of power that Westerners and
primitive artists have in the process of art production, distribution, and
appreciation. This list of ways in which the West controls primitive art
is derived from Price (1989:68–70).

1. Its value is determined by the discriminating eye of the
   Westerner.
2. Museums and collectors set their own priorities on the life and
   death of primitive art objects, that is, whether they are "in" or
   "out."
3. Connoisseurs interpret meaning and significance.
4. Western experts have money and means of communication to
   establish favorites.
5. Experts determine the nature of artistic production in vitually
   every part of the world in the final decades of the twentieth
   century.

Those who have the power to define, to name, do not hesitate to do so.
Those on the other end too often begin to conform to the images assigned
to them, as when art is made to conform to outsider expectations of
tourists.

When Western art is displayed in a Western museum for a Western audience there is less need for detailed labels decribing context,
motive, and design, because all elements are from the same cultural tra-

dition, and assumptions can be made about what already is known. But how much should we explain an art display from a tradition different from our own? More enlightened gallery directors today appear to be trying to elevate the status of some primitive art by reducing contextual display and label explanation (Price 1989:82–99), thinking that any viewer will appreciate its intrinsic beauty. It can stand alone. Conversely, too much contextualization throws it back into the category of an ethnographic museum, which does a better job of contextualizing it but removes it from the realm of art.

It is unlikely that the "primitive" artist will be asked to rule on what is a masterpiece in either culture. But leaving primitive art decontextualized leaves too much room for myths and misunderstandings to operate freely. Contextualization, on the other hand, can re-educate the eye. Because such art is so easily misunderstood, fuller explanation might be the better course, leaving decisions about whether a work should be viewed as art or artifact for later.

Tourist arts (Graburn 1976) offer particularly interesting examples of culture contact and confused perspectives. Australian Aborigines painted their bodies and sometimes the bark of their dwellings in the service of ritual. They did not sell their bark paintings aboriginally (Williams 1976:271). Missionaries at Yirrkala on the northeast coast of Arnhem Land in Australia introduced to these hunters and gatherers the idea of developing self-sufficiency in a cash economy based on the sale of traditional arts. Missionaries sold the bark paintings to Museums and universities, but with the stipulation that all work had to be genuine with no innovation (p. 274). By 1964, missionaries in the area were issuing certificates of authenticity with sales of aboriginal artwork (p. 277).

Although there was a strain toward producing artwork that would be aesthetically pleasing to the white buyer (Williams 1976:272)—particularly with respect to its fit and finish—the Aboriginal artists responded, and there seemed to be a restoration of community pride in the fact that outsiders would purchase their art. In fact, what was happening was that contemporary art was performing a traditional function: ". . . to reinforce and to enhance an important aspect of traditional culture, and the values it expresses" (p. 282). Youths who wanted to be artists had first to learn the traditional lore and values—which stand as law—of the community.

Purists would like to see native art for sale to outsiders certified for authenticity, with no innovation, and untainted by Western values, so that tourists know that they are getting the real thing. Those who hold the opposite view, emphasizing continuing adaptation, would like to see people free to innovate and to draw on their traditions to sustain them as they make a transition into the modern world. From bark paintings, some Aboriginal artists have gone to acrylic on canvas and applications of traditional viewpoints to interpreting their contemporary circumstances. Both purist and adaptational views surface in the example of Aboriginal art, as well as tourist art in general. Should we keep people on museum display, preserving some imagined original state, or permit them to enter the modern world? As Price points out, however, the power differential works against traditional artists in the contemporary world, although some today have works in national museums and fine art galleries.

The tension between purist and adaptational views is mirrored in ideas of preservation and conservation. Preservation supports authenticating the past, an attitude which carries with it valuing the traditions of people whose culture has been denigrated for centuries. This view, however, denies a community the value of continuing to adapt to a changing world. The idea of conservation (Hufford 1994) allows for both tradition and change. The conservation approach, like the adaptational view, permits the local community to adapt its traditional perspectives to its contemporary experience. Tradition in this view becomes a vibrant, living fund of knowledge, rather than a dead museum piece. The art of the Runa (Ecuador) illustrates the adaptive value of art as well as the value of applied anthropology (Whitten and Whitten 1988). Traditional pottery and carved balsa wood forest creatures both sustain key traditional beliefs and values as well as make statements on contemporary events. They also bring in badly needed cash. The Runa feel that they are exercising some control over the pace and direction of change. They are neither passive nor powerless pawns in the modern world.

The Myth of Africa

Stereotypes of native peoples can be widely disseminated through popular literature. In their study of some five hundred books of fiction and nonfiction on Africa, Hammond and Jablow (1977) discovered that the literary image of Africa, beginning with the period of slavery, is a "fantasy of a continent and a people that never were and could never be" (p. 14). Further,

> African behavior, institutions, and character were not merely disparaged but presented as the negation of all human decencies. African religions were vile superstitions; governments but cruel despotism; polygyny was not marriage, but the expression of innate lusts. The shift to such pejorative comment was due in large measure to the effects of the slave trade. A vested interest in the slave trade produced a literature of devaluation, and since the slave trade was under attack, the most derogatory writing about Africans came from its literary defenders. (Hammond and Jablow 1970:23)

In response, the antislavery literary figures set about to create a new Africa based on the idea of the Noble Savage, who was, in this case, the African prince or princess, who looked more European, shared British values, and was representative of royal lines. The real tragedy was that royalty had been reduced to servile status (Hammond and Jablow 1977:27).

Africa became a metaphor for all that was dark, animalistic, and horrific. It stood for the dark interior of the civilized person with whom one had to come to grips. It was a land of timelessness. Africa tested one's character. Men went to Africa to become men, to maintain their values and their discipline in the face of unimaginable hardship, and to overcome ordeals. Africa serves as a convenient example of ethnocentric projection, but the same themes were common throughout all of the colonial world.

But the modern world continues to have a voracious appetite for similar stereotypes. In 1956, Elizabeth Marshall Thomas wrote a popular book on the San people of southern Africa, entitled *The Harmless People*. The book, buttressed by an educational film, *The Hunters*, educated two generations of college students on the people of this region. The educational film and book depicted the San as both harmless and charming, and living a life that represented an earlier stage of cultural development. Students may well still be receiving that message. In 1981, a film which included the San, *The Gods Must Be Crazy*, became immensely popular throughout the world. It depicted, stereotypically, the San as living in child-like innocence and primitive affluence free of the woes of civilization. Its impact on the San, or Bushmen as they are more popularly known, was disastrous as film crews descended upon them with great regularity. The film is credited with adding impetus to a push for a Bushmanland as a game reserve (Gordon 1992:1).

Some San live near the Tswana where Marianne Alverson received her lesson in reading the sands (see chapter 1). They have a justified image for being excellent trackers, but their skills, which some outsiders regard as superhuman, are learned, their eye educated. Their skill is not necessarily to be admired because it tends to be closely associated in the minds of outsiders with people of animalistic nature; the myth dictates that only a creature close to nature could be so acutely attuned to its natural environment. The supposed fact that they are "natural trackers" (as opposed to learning to adapt) accentuates their difference from civilized people.

The San themselves have no umbrella name for themselves, but recognize only individual groups. In his study of the "Bushman Myth," Robert Gordon focuses on the "the colonizer's image of them and the consequences of that image for people assumed to be Bushmen" (1992:4). Like Africa itself, the San have been rediscovered by governments, churches, news media, scientists, and lay people at various times according to their own agendas. Consequently the San have not always been the harmless people. Because of their learned skill, the San were heavily recruited into the South African Defense Force (SADF) during the 1980s to help them fight a guerilla war against the South-West People's Organization (SWAPO), a militant nationalist group (Gordon 1992:2), for which the San were paid. Thus, the San, who had few means of acquiring cash, could use their tracking skills to do so.

Early in the history of contact, they successfully fought against a variety of intruders. Gordon (1992) observes that they have "the longest, most valiant, if costly, record of resistance to Colonialism" (p. 7). Indeed, the word, San, proposed by those who believe that "Bushmen" is sexist and racist, more likely means "bandits" (pp. 5–6). It would be an accurate label for their historical and violent struggle on the frontier.

The San also have resisted Christian missionary efforts. Missionaries say that the San have been unable to distance themselves from their old culture, citing particularly their reliance on the trance dance (Gordon 1992:210–12). Anthropologists, on the other hand, stress the functional meaning of the trance dance to reaffirm kinship bonds and to be perhaps the most effective mechanism that the San have to cope with change (p. 12).

As elsewhere, outsiders draw contrast between themselves and the San—wild natives against civilized peoples. Untamed or undomesticated, like animals, they are unlikely to be assimilated into civilization. Their distinctiveness has been premised on their different physique, and different culture and values, and has supplied outsiders with a constant source of myth making for their own purposes. As Gordon (1992:212) points out, these were not descriptive categories, but a principle of colonization. Throughout colonization, scientific books, and popular films, the difference between them and us is stressed rather than our commonality.

These are not isolated, harmless, backward, or affluent people; they are, in Gordon's terms, people who live in a state of "integrated rural poverty" plagued by illness, hunger and powerlessness (p. 3). They are very much a part of the modern world system and their nation, but increasingly becoming a dependent "underclass" in a cash economy.

Today, native peoples are increasingly resisting these images and myths, as well as striving to gain more political and economic power, and thus hoping to secure a better life for themselves. In the following section we note some of these efforts.

NATIVE RESURGENCE AND POLITICAL ACTIONS

After World War II, Native Americans began to speak strongly and act forcefully to bring public attention to their cause. In the 1960s they staged a "fish-in" in the Pacific Northwest to assert their treaty rights. They seized Alcatraz in 1969, seized the Bureau of Indian Affairs headquarters in 1979, and shortly after they seized Wounded Knee. Wounded Knee is highly symbolic because on December 28, 1890, approximately 100 Sioux warriors and 250 women and children surrendered to the U.S. Seventh Cavalry. They were being moved to a reservation, but twenty miles short of their destination, violence erupted as soldiers searched tents for weapons. Men, women, and children were massacred, with very few escaping (Cornell 1988:3).

These seizures mark some of the important milestones in Native American efforts to revitalize themselves and their culture and to make their way in a world in which they have had little power. Cornell observes:

> Groups act not only *within* limits set by forces beyond their control, including their own distinctive histories. They also act *upon* those limits. In the process they may remake themselves and the world in which they live, and thereby the conditions under which they act. (Cornell 1988:8)

Native Americans have been remaking themselves and acting on limits particularly over the past three decades. Moreover, they have come together more as a single unit to amplify the impact of their actions. The stereotypical and dominant treatment of Native Americans required a response based on a common, supratribal consciousness (Cornell 1988). Native Americans did not use inclusive terms to describe themselves until it became politically necessary to present a common front. Like the San, they tended to think of themselves as individual groups until political reality forced united action.

In his popular book, *Custer Died for Your Sins* (1969), Vine Deloria, Jr., captured the essence of white-Indian perceptions of each other in clear and simple terms.

> Because the Negro labored, he was considered a draft animal. Because the Indian occupied large areas of land, he was considered a wild animal. (p. 8)

> Whenever Indian land was needed, the whites pictured the tribes as wasteful people who refused to develop their natural resources. Because the Indians did not "use" their lands, argued many land promoters, the lands should be taken away and given to people who knew what to do with them. (p. 10)

But Indians have been cursed above all other people in history, Indians have anthropologists. (p. 78)

It has been said of missionaries that when they arrived they had only the Book and we had the land. Now we have the Book and they have the land. (p. 79)

Native peoples of South America also have acted decisively to adapt to their current circumstances while attempting to preserve their traditional ways as much as possible. In recent years, jarring images in the popular press of feathered and painted Indians wielding videocameras have jolted the stereotyped images of non-native viewers. One such group, the Kayapo of Brazil, took up the camera partly as a way of documenting their agreements with national officials and other parties, such as gold miners who often renege on their promises. They have been skillful users of modern media to gain attention and push demands as have others in Amazonia like the Xavante. Some Kayapo have become accountants in order to keep their own books on their receipts from gold miners who work on their land, access to which they tightly control, and take a percentage of the gold that is shipped out.

The resurgence of native peoples in the Amazon Basin is led by those who have had the longest contact, and therefore more time to recover from the ravages of early contact, with Westerners. These people never wished to be Western and resisted until their population recovered and until they learned more of the world that dominated them. They now see that they must deal, as Cornell said, with the world as given them, and to remake themselves. This means educating teachers, medical personnel, lawyers, and accountants and honing the skills to manipulate modern media to their advantage.

Similarly, the Shuar, "headhunters," of Ecuador have teamed with their other Jivaroan-speaking neighbors to create a *federaccion* which has become quite successful (Bodley 1990:160–62). They have operated a radio station since 1968, published a bilingual newspaper, and produced their own film on their traditional ways. At the same time, their culture has changed significantly over the years. They believe that they have generally changed for the better, but more important, they feel that they control the pace and direction of change.

These groups are now linking-up internationally with other groups in Canada, the Philippines, and Australia. Such groups as IWGIA (International Work Groups for Indigenous Affairs), World Council of Indigenous Peoples, Cultural Survival, and Survival International are supported additionally by private persons, churches, and the United Nations (Bodley 1990:177).

CONCLUSION

We can agree with Kluckhohn that looking at others is like looking into a mirror and getting a fresh view of ourselves, but we should question whether or not the mirror metaphor, alone, is any longer a sufficiently useful one. Adding the voices of others would capture the more strident spirit of today.

The doctrine of racial inferiority accompanied the age of European colonization of most of the world, and it supported a campaign of domination and exploitation. The Europeans had a vested interest in defining and categorizing indigenous peoples. Even the seeming altruistic ideal of the Noble Savage served more the political philosophies of the Europeans regarding the European state, than it did those so classified. Native peoples were twice defeated. They everywhere fought and resisted European incursions, but were eventually defeated by force and disease. In the aftermath, they were usually defeated once more by the insidious forces of religion, education, and consumerism. Myths about darkest Africa, misunderstandings of primitive art, and the distorted images conveyed to us by popular media tell us more about ourselves than they do about other people. In recent decades, native and minority peoples, formerly relatively voiceless, have found their voices and taken active steps to control their future.

Chapter Five

Mirrors and Voices

In the previous chapters we established the fact of our common humanity, explained how diversity develops from local adaptations, noted the responses of insiders to the incursions of outsiders, and examined our ethnocentrism. Now, we return to our earlier discussion of field experience and culture shock. We do so in order to avoid the shallow, cookbook approach to making sense of human diversity and to achieve instead a much greater depth in our grasp of the complexities of cross-cultural understanding.

HISTORICAL BACKGROUND TO FIELDWORK

Anthropologists bring to issues of human diversity over a century of experience in professional fieldwork. However, the transition from amateur to professional anthropologist covered several decades. In England, Edward B. Tylor (1871) noted the importance of obtaining quality data from the field, and W.H.R. Rivers contributed the genealogical method (a method of recording kinship relationships) in 1910. Bronislaw Malinowski wrote an early and influential guide to doing fieldwork in 1922. In North America, Lewis Henry Morgan gathered genealogical material among the Iroquois in the middle 1800s. The Bureau of American Ethnology, under the leadership of J. W. Powell, had already initiated a series of field studies that preceded Franz Boas' ([1940] 1966) vigorous advocacy of fieldwork at the turn of the century. Nevertheless, it was Boas and his many influential students who secured the place of field experience in American anthropology during the first half of this century. Boas saw the task of collecting data firsthand as the crucial basis of scientific thought, and therefore as the basis for a scientific anthropology.

In a remarkable paradox, professional British and North American anthropologists stressed the supreme importance of fieldwork—to this day very few Ph.D. candidates, in fact, escape "ordeal by fieldwork"—but gave little formal direction about how one in fact actually did it. The experience was mystifying not just for novices, but remained largely a mute topic among seasoned veterans as well. Anthropology's myth was that doctoral students suddenly packed up their cameras and notebooks and went off to an exotic place to return a year or two later with a body of data which they then proceeded to "write up" for professional publications. They all seemed to have good experiences and got along well with "their people." Sometimes, individuals would have their health threatened by serious illness, but this seemed the only real source of difficulty. The principal methodological strategy of the discipline, participant observation, was not a topic for formal discussion or critical commentary. In 1967, however, Malinowski's field diary was published, revealing that the actual conditions of his field research were very much different from the ideal procedure he set down in 1922. This fact sparked the first lively debate on the nature of fieldwork.

Already there were rumblings of discontent with the secrecy and mystique of field research, and Malinowski's diary added more fuel to some of the controversies that were beginning to smolder at the time. Until the late 1960s only a few ethnographers permitted the public or the profession to know the actual conditions under which they worked. One exception was Laura Bohannan's (published under the name of Elenore Smith Bowen whose quote began the first chapter) scintillating, fictionalized account of her fieldwork in Africa, *Return to Laughter* ([1954] 1964), in which many of the common problems of working in another culture were described in frank and painstaking detail. Over a decade later other publications such as *Marginal Natives* (Freilich, 1968) began to appear containing informed discussions of methodological and ethical issues in fieldwork. Valentine (1968), *Culture and Poverty*, criticized on both theoretical and methodological grounds a number of urban poverty studies. Principal among his complaints is that too many investigators of the urban poor had no direct and prolonged experience with their impoverished subjects. Golde's *Women in the Field* appeared in 1970 to address gender as one of the important variables influencing the fieldwork experience. In the short period of five years, fieldwork received more critical scrutiny than in all the preceding decades combined.

The exposure of fieldwork as less than idealistic was followed by initiatives casting anthropology as a neocolonial representative of the established political and economic interests of the dominant West, in spite of the discipline's claim to the contrary, that it was merely pursuing matters of scientific interest. A national climate of radical protest and pressure for change affected campuses throughout the 1960s and into the following decade. Much of this protest was mustered by and in support of minority groups in the United States, but spread to include oppressed native residents of formerly colonized areas around the world; both minorities and native peoples were common anthropological subjects. As noted previously, many of the issues are discussed in Hymes (1969).

These political protests were aimed at an audience larger than anthropology, for they called into question the general validity of a value-free, objective social science. Marxists reminded social scientists that they too were limited by their place in the stream of history, that they saw the world from a limited point of view. Suddenly, it seemed impossible to conduct unbiased research among other peoples, including the poor and the powerless of our own country. The view that a completely value-free social science is not possible predominates most, but not all, of social science thought today. Yet, we continue to strive for the elusive ideal of objectivity, knowing that we will fall short of the ideal.

Where Malinowski's diary made ordinary fieldwork less than ideal, the climate of revolution in the late 1960s cast doubt on the scientific purity of anthropology in general as well as undermining the value of firsthand observation. Anthropologists were admonished to reinvent anthropology (Hymes 1969). Field researchers were encouraged to be even more self-critical, or *reflexive*, to probe ever deeper into the very nature of their field experience and to discover in themselves more subtle forms of bias. Social scientists were often invited to go the extra step, to be social advocates. It should be noted for the record that early anthropologists such as Boas and Herskovits spoke out eloquently and frequently against racism and other forms of bias at a time when it was not popular to do so.

In the 1980s, a flood of "confessional ethnographies" appeared in which fieldworkers stripped aside some of the mystique of life in the field. Ethnographers became more sensitive to the kind of intellectual and emotional baggage they brought with them to the field site. Some of these works were inspired by literary influences where observers interpret cultures as if they were texts; that is, a culture can, like a text, be interpreted or "read" effectively in many ways by a variety of professional observers (Marcus and Fischer 1986). From this perspective there is no single, objective, authoritative, scientific truth, but various plausible interpretations. This stance is associated with a widespread interdisciplinary movement called postmodern thought, which rejects many of the assumptions of a positivist fact-finding science such as Boas imagined anthropology would be. Many who find value in such views, however, warn that they do not support cursory and sloppy field research (Brady 1991), nor do they encourage violations of the standards of professional anthropology, regardless of their particular theoretical preference.

Today, most ethnographers, regardless of their theoretical perspective, are much more sensitive to the quality of the discourse between themselves and those they observe, and more alert to how the circumstances of their experience influence their explanations, or interpretations, of research results.

We have thus far cited many of the recent ethnographies espousing the new awareness. They have the power to convey to us in striking and highly personal detail the raw and messy side of fieldwork; they are personal testimonies to the hold culture has on us, the elusiveness of the goal of understanding the other, and our personal perseverance in the face of grave doubts and uncertainty. Although most of us will never do anthropological fieldwork, we cannot say for sure anymore where we will be living and working in the future. If we are not working abroad, we will increasingly encounter substantial cultural differences within our own country. We use the fieldwork process here as a pedagogical tool by which to unravel some of the enigmas of engaging another culture.

THE SHOCK OF THE NEW

At this point, we return to examine more closely the theme of our opening chapter, culture shock. Although most successful field researchers have a high tolerance for ambiguity and uncertainty, they, too, suffer from the shock of the new. As Michael Agar writes,

> The shock comes from a sudden immersion in the lifeways of a group different from yourself. Suddenly, you do not know how to interpret the stream of motions and noises that surround you. You have no idea what is expected of you. Many of the assumptions that form the bedrock of your existence are mercilessly ripped out from under you. The more you cling to them, the less you will understand about the people with whom you work. (1980:50)

Even inexperienced anthropologists are expected to know quite a bit about how cultures work, and partly because of these expectations their initial frustrations can be especially difficult to handle. In addition, fieldworkers are usually under time constraints, the time available never seems adequate to the task at hand. William Mitchell writes the following letter of frustration while in New Guinea.

> I'm spending weeks trying to figure out what any slow eight year old has known for several years. Now, I know why the older generation of anthropologists never accepted anyone as a bonafide anthropologist until they have been humbled by a primitive culture.

It's the analog of a didactic psychoanalysis; you're never the same again. You've been peeled, stripped and reduced to the feeling of a Total Ignoramous. The level of stupidity at which I operate—even after five months here—is absolutely appalling. And I'm not a bad anthropologist, but the monumental shifts it takes to apprehend the local version of reality sometimes unhinges me a bit. After all, I've usually been able to *feel* what was going on about me even if I didn't know the details of what was happening. Now I've been humbled on that one, too! (1987:104)

Fieldworkers can prepare intellectually for shock, but as Mitchell's letter shows, there is little they can do to prepare emotionally for the experience. Shock comes in unexpected forms. Indeed, anthropologists frequently experience reverse shock upon returning home from an extended stay in the field. This is an experience for which, early in their career, they are totally unprepared.

More important than the experience of shock, however, is what we make of it. Knowing that people usually work through shock is helpful. And knowing that it will occur and knowing the symptoms forewarns us. Working through shock is aided by a good sense of humor, especially the ability to laugh at oneself (at least silently). Learning the local culture sufficiently well to predict the course of daily behavior routinizes your life, and rewards you with a sense of settling in. As you begin to learn the language you begin to increase the number of your acquaintances. When you begin to know a few insiders as individuals you personalize the experience. Familiarity establishes human anchor points in a sea of strange faces. Remembering that your hosts are also going through a period of adjustment to your presence should take some of the sting out of your own discomfort and encourage your patience. That they need to fit your presence into their lives is important to figuring out what they are up to. They also need time to know you as a person. They may be wary of your intentions, and generally suspicious as to why you are there, so it may take some time for them to trust you.

Anthropologists know that various episodes of shock—it is not necessarily a one-time experience and it may come early, or late, or in the middle, although likely to come earlier than later—will challenge them to understand more about their own culture as well as the other culture. They know, too, that shock will tell them something important about their host culture. In other words, we should use the shocks and crises of fieldwork to advance understanding which also will enhance personal adjustment. Mitchell (1987:78), although humbled at first by feelings of inadequacy, advanced personally and anthropologically when he learned why there was so much trouble over his method of paying porters in New Guinea. He had given a lump sum to the two men who had organized his move to the village. They redistributed it to the porters. But the porters were angry that they did not receive more. Because of their discontent, he discovered quickly how egalitarian Wape culture really is by observing their own method of distributing their pay, which was more Western than he expected. He then followed their way.

The ethnocentric view that one's own way of life is the best, the most natural, lurks always in our unconscious mind, and is exposed only when challenged. Because of the abuses of amateur, armchair anthropologists of the past century, professional anthropologists invented the idea of *cultural relativism* to guard against our natural tendency to prejudge and to drag our own cultural baggage to the field with us. Cultural relativism advocates understanding other ways of life in their contexts. Anthropologists try to find out what is, not what should be from our point of view. We pursue the goal of withholding judgment and striving for an accurate understanding of a culture on its own terms. Melville Herskovits (1973), who wrote a great deal about cultural relativism, observed that this precept calls for a "tough-minded" attitude to try to understand the native point of view, without allowing your own to distort your observations or your conclusions about them. A scientific anthropology should be as objective as possible, in spite of the problems in actually attaining the ideal.

Unfortunately, the public often misunderstands cultural relativism to advocate amorality and behavioral anarchy. Anthropology has probably allowed the public to think so by not doing a better job of explaining the precept. By insisting that a culture should be understood in terms of its own logic, anthropologists seem to be saying that anything goes, there are no universal standards of behavior, and thus we leave the door open to misunderstanding. The historical intention of Boas and Herskovits was to shift focus from the grand comparative schemes of the amateurs to the unbiased observation of cultures in their local contexts. They wanted to collect unbiased facts by first-hand contact.

Anthropologists know that human societies cannot exist in the face of behavioral anarchy and amorality. Advocating such would encourage our own demise. The role of culture and morality is to guide human behavior so that we work sufficiently well together to survive in groups. Anthropologists do not condone all forms of behavior simply because they observed them in the field. To report them is not to advocate them. As a methodological strategy, rather than moral stance, cultural relativism stands as a somewhat imperfect ideal because while it awards to others an intrinsic human value that they have not always been given, and is intended to combat ethnocentrism, it does not deal well with the source of bias—our own culture. We need to be tough-minded about ourselves and our culture as well as others'. This is why entering into productive dialogues, the give-and-take of fieldwork, and being reflexive is so important.

THE DIALOGUE OF FIELDWORK

Anthropology's special contribution to science is its combination of perspective and method. (1) *We control bias by referring to the real world in which a group of people live*, and (2) *we control the quality of data by entering that world to learn it first-hand*. To these two principles, we now can add a third. (3) *Anthropologists increasingly see fieldwork as a dialogue between cultures*. Notice that two of these principles restate those introduced in chapter 3. The third principle is the subject of this chapter.

Anthropologists are commonly known to the public simply as those who study other cultures. But there are, as we know from our discussion of culture shock, always two cultures involved. A dialogue recognizes two essential dimensions of fieldwork that were too-often missing in the ideal objective observer, or positivist, approach: (1) it takes into account the cultural baggage of the observer; and, (2) it recognizes the effect of the observer on the culture being observed and what the observed learns from the observer. It may include as well the critical comments that the observed wishes to make about the observer's culture, a theme of the previous chapter.

Observer and observed are observing each other and each is trying to make sense of the other in terms of his own culture. Anthropologists ask scores of questions, some of which may never have been asked before. Thus, the insiders also learn something of their own culture even if only to reaffirm it in the face of probing questions asked by an outsider. Rabinow (1977:116–21) reports an example from Morocco. He and an informant-assistant, Malik, were working on a profile of the socioeconomic variations present in the village. Rabinow suggested they examine Malik's socioeconomic status, but as they did so Malik became uncomfortable.

> The "facts" which were emerging did not correspond to his cultural categories. Moroccan villagers are not in the habit of totaling up their parcels of land, calculating their combined holdings, comparing them with the rising and falling prices of goods, and making systematic and quantitative comparisons with their neighbors. Nor do they understand their village conceptually in terms of socioeconomic strata. . . .
>
> Malik began to see that there was disparity between his self-image and my classification system. (Rabinow 1977:117–18)

For Malik, the local culture dictated that things were either going well or not going well. That was the only concern the people had. The anthropologist's questions, and reorganization of the village in outsider terms, made Malik reflect on his own circumstances from a new perspective. He was challenged, and it made him uncomfortable. Because Rabinow reflected on his informant's response to his question, rather than just fixing on the hard facts it yielded, he was able to reach a new level of understanding.

Discovering the extent to which one is guided by one's own culture comes in bits and pieces. The dimensions of our bias cannot be discovered all at once in their complexity. One way of suggesting this process of discovery is to think of ethnocentrism as having two levels. *Explicit ethnocentrism* refers to those viewpoints derived from our own culture of which we are aware—the surface layer. Being conscious of these explicit biases does not necessarily mean that we discard them, but at least we recognize them and can talk about them. *Implicit ethnocentrism* refers to the unconscious biases that we hold as a result of internalizing a culture. They are unexamined attitudes and values, habits of thinking, and ways of feeling. They are the concealed inner layers of our culture that we discover with surprise if we discover them at all. The work of Stoller and Feld on the senses, cited earlier, are examples of implicit ethnocentrism—the West's tendency to give higher value to vision over the other senses.

In the language of science, fieldwork falls into the category of the *logic of discovery*. In contrast, scientific reports, including the old-style ethnographies, are usually seen as reconstructions of research and as reports of the results. They are examples of *reconstructed logic*, a formal report that does not include the complete details of how, in fact, the study was done. The report of a lab experiment might leave out the fact of dirty test tubes or potentially important ambient temperature variations because it did not seem important to the findings. While most such reconstructions have no significant effect on the findings, the potential remains that they might. Work in the field is far less controlled than in a laboratory, so it makes good sense to be alert to how field conditions might bias results. Ethnographic reports until recently said very little about how anthropologists actually discovered another culture, and how the conditions of discovery might affect their findings. They maintained the fiction of completely objective observation. Thus we knew more about fieldwork results than we did about fieldwork as a logic of discovery. Malinowski's diary, never intended for publication, was for this reason a revelation. Through his frustrations, sexual desires, and biases, the messy side of field experience was exposed in steamy detail. Anthropologists now write more frankly about the contingencies of their discovery of another culture so that their findings can be better evaluated in light of their actual experience.

Alverson's report on how she learned about hosting and serving kadi (see chapter 1) falls into the realm of discovery. She describes how both sides came to understand a bit about themselves as well as the other. In the traditional ethnographic report she would have simply reported what the Tswana custom is with respect to hosting and serving kadi, a bit of reconstructed logic, without the details of their strained interaction and her initial confusion. Because she did report the details, we see better the dialogue between her and the Tswana and the process by which she learned their culture.

OBSERVATION AND PARTICIPATION

Michael Jackson, an advocate of radical empiricism, which stresses participating in events rather than just taking notes on them (at least during the event in question), states:

> The importance of this view for anthropology is that it stresses the ethnographer's *interactions* with those he or she lives with and studies, while urging us to clarify the ways in which our knowledge is grounded in our practical, personal, and participatory experience in the field as much as our detached observations. Unlike traditional empiricism which draws a definite boundary between observer and observed, between method and object, radical empiricism denies the validity of such cuts and makes the *interplay* between these domains the focus of interest. (1989:3)

Taking notes without real participation maintains distance between the observed and the observer. Living in a culture is better than not being there, but living in a culture and dispassionately taking notes is a limited form of participation.

No one can say precisely what the proper mix of observation and participation is, because the answer depends on a number of variables including the nature of the problem, personality of the observer, and the local situation. In the past, the issue has been addressed in the rather simple and dichotomous terms of maintaining objective distance and avoiding emotional involvement, that is, being a scientist or "going native" and losing objectivity. Michael Harner (1968) believed that he did not properly understand Shuar (known then as Jivaro) religious ideas, and that the key to further discovery lay in his ingesting, as do the Shuar, hallucinogenic drugs. He, in fact, took the drugs and later reported in detail on his experiences and how they advanced his understanding of Shuar religious beliefs. Here, Harner measured the probability of gaining crucial knowledge against the "loss of objectivity" and "going native." One would have to decide on the wisdom of his choice by judging the quality of his report. Twenty years earlier, Harner would more likely have reported the results of his research into Shuar religion without discussing how he came to acquire the insider's view of it.

Jackson (1989) makes two important points. First, there might be a critical difference between taking notes while observing a native canoe being constructed, and making the canoe yourself. Without actually participating, you may or may not be able to report accurately and completely the values, motivation, skill, and effort that accompany an observed task. Myerson (1990:156–57) worked in the potato fields of a Andean village, and later tried her hand at weaving (p. 163). Both experiences left her with a new perspective on these fundamental activities which, had she not attempted them, might otherwise have escaped her attention as worthy of further study.

Second, Jackson suggests that the essence of fieldwork lies in interaction. No anthropologist, regardless of her theoretical focus, would disagree with the idea that interaction and significant participation are the bases for effective fieldwork, although she might not embrace the whole of Jackson's approach. He is simply making the point that observation cannot pass as participation. He is less concerned than Laura Bohannan was in the first chapter about becoming too involved and losing objectivity.

Response Effects

We participate in culture largely as *social persons*, rather than on the basis of individual identity. Each of us, for example, occupies a role and status (actually, a set of roles and statuses). *Response effects* refers to the measurable differences in interview data resulting from the sociocultural characteristics of interviewers, informants, and the settings in which interviews take place. Whether or not one is formally interviewing, or just carrying on conversations, sociocultural characteristics influence the nature and results of these talks.

One particularly important variable is the real or perceived power difference between interviewer and the respondent. How sensitive are the data sought by the interviewer? What repercussions does the informant risk in interacting with the interviewer? What sort of symbolic significance does the interview and the setting have for the participants?

Another way of emphasizing social context is to say that the participants in a dialogue—insider and outsider—are both *socially situated* in a culture. Although the Panare at first had difficulty placing Dumont ([1978] 1992) in their culture, they eventually found a place for him as a brother to one of his informants. To some degree this change in status changed the nature of the dialogue between them. At the end of his fieldwork he was somewhat differently "situated" than he was at the beginning. But he was still an outsider, a master identity that he could not shake entirely even as a "brother," and which continued to influence the discovery process, that is, his access to information. In writing his interpretations of the Panare, Dumont tried to consider what kind of an effect he had on them, but he could never know its full extent. He reports that he was never sure just how seriously the Panare took his role as "brother" ([1978] 1992:94).

Cultures vary in how much *role flexibility* they permit either outsiders or insiders. Both insider and outsider statuses are at issue in the case of some Arab women. Arab women with doctoral degrees in anthropology from U.S. universities experience varying degrees of freedom and role flexibility when they return to their own culture to conduct research. Arab cultures are characterized by a high degree of gender segregation—gender identity produces a master structural constraint on behavior—but Arab female anthropologists may be able to mitigate these constraints because of their education, their social class, their ambiguous "foreign" status, or even their place in a life-cycle stage (Altorki and Fawzi El-Sohl 1984). Additional local contingencies influence the degree of freedom with which they can work.

Rapport

The successful execution of research among humans is often said to depend upon good *rapport*, that is, a productive relationship based on a certain level of acceptance and harmony between the researcher and the informant. Rapport does not refer to a warm fuzzy state enveloping the participants, but to an effective working relationship between them. The success of such a relationship seems to rest most commonly on a basic recognition and acceptance of the human qualities of another person. But it also rests frequently on the manipulations and vested interests of both researcher and informant. While a workable rapport is in fact usually achieved in the field, it is often somewhat tenuous and dependent on other contingencies. For example, early informants are likely to be marginal in their own culture and the fieldworker must then proceed with caution so that she will not alienate herself from the mainstream. Equally important is to be wary of internal factions, for they cannot always be avoided and can curtail your freedom of movement if you are caught between them. Status aside, rapport can certainly depend upon the individual personalities involved. It is, however, often difficult initially for the fieldworker to separate role behavior and class factors from personality characteristics.

Needless to say, if a fieldworker cannot suspend judgment or control her explicit biases, she will not build a good rapport with informants. Thus, the fieldworker will not be able to get at her implicit biases and to work toward constructing a satisfactory knowledge of the culture. The fieldworker stands in the path of her own development.

Beginning to recognize both social and individual persons marks progress toward alleviating culture shock and building an understanding of that culture. Recognized and valued faces emerge from the crowd of strangers whom one encounters in the early days of fieldwork. At this point the worker is establishing good rapport. She then might enter a stage where *counter-transference* takes place. This term draws an analogy between psychological testing and certain aspects of the fieldwork process (Devereux 1980). The culture under investigation is like an ink blot on a projective test (the Rorschach test) upon which the fieldworker, as subject, can project her needs and anxieties. For example, the fieldworker may have developed a relationship of dependency with a person or a family which has been particularly helpful and sympathetic, and consequently projected to that person or family deeply felt feelings of closeness and kinship. The others might or might not actually share that feeling of closeness. The worker might begin to idealize their personalities and actions even in her professional interpretations of the host culture. Dumont ([1978] 1992:94) makes this point in questioning how much of a brother he really is. Has he over-estimated, romanticized, the significance of the relationship? Counter-transference represents yet another level of the cultural and psychological dynamic of the fieldwork exchange. But it is an experience that any traveler may have when cared for in another culture.

Objective Distance and Repositioning

Michael Jackson's radical empiricism is calculated to narrow the objective distance between observer and observed. The celebrated social science stance of neutrality and objectivity, however, has never really existed except in the ideal. "If distance has certain arguable advantages, so too does closeness, and both have their deficits. Yet classical social science has enclosed the former with excessive virtue, and the latter with excessive vice" (Rosaldo 1989:169). Distancing risks reducing the raw data of everyday life to bloodless routine. Stoller (1989) makes the same point when he criticizes the ethnography that only defines and visualizes, leaving us blind to some experiences of others. After years of working with the Ilongot, Rosaldo unintentionally "repositions" himself to see the Ilongot motivation for headhunting from a different perspective.

> Not until some fourteen years after first recording the terse Ilongot statement about grief and a headhunter's rage did I begin to grasp its overwhelming force. For years I thought that more verbal elaboration (which was not forthcoming) or another analytical level (which remained elusive) could explain older men's motives for headhunting. Only after being repositioned through a devastating loss of my own could I better grasp that Ilongot men mean precisely

what they say when they describe the anger in bereavement as the source of their desire to cut off human heads. (Rosaldo 1989:31)

Rosaldo (p. 10) does not contend here that he knows exactly how Ilongot feel (although his anger is partially like theirs), only that the agony of his own loss makes him realize that objective distance tends to remove emotions as motivation in the rawness of daily life. The distanced perspective reduces humanity to grieving for ritual and social structural reasons, not because of their profound pain. But they do feel the pain of loss. Because of his recognition of common ground, Rosaldo believes that he has raised his dialogue with the Ilongot to a new level of insight.

Note that Rosaldo is careful not to assume that he does know exactly how the Ilongot feel, only that he has a new appreciation, a new insight on how they might feel. This is an important distinction and a good place to consider briefly the notion of finding empathy with others. Humans do have the ability to put themselves in the place of others, to appreciate their dilemmas and emotions. Social systems depend to some degree on our being able to form some empathy with others in a family, a team, an organization. Yet, imagining that you understand how someone else feels carries with it the obvious danger that you may not really understand at all, that you have in fact misidentified the situation by projecting too much of yourself into the situation. While you may be extending yourself in good faith to try to see the world from the other person's point of view, you are still subject to your own personal and cultural preconceptions. We cannot say that empathy is not a goal, but we should say proceed with caution.

Extending the dialogue beyond his personal experience, Rosaldo uses his repositioning to see North American culture in a fresh light. He reflects that North Americans would not generally be in a good position to understand grief and death because their culture is largely silent about such things. Mainstream North American culture denies death and grief, and this denial leaves its participants unprepared to cope with these events in other cultures. Many of us are, according to Rosaldo, culturally, emotionally, and therefore conceptually, distanced from these facts of life because of our own culture. Yet, bereavement is universal no matter how or to what degree it is expressed. How could he not recognize beneath the Ilongot cultural form the drama of attachment and loss that plagues us all? It is not precisely the same grief, but it is nonetheless grief.

Taking the approach of anthropologists such as Rosaldo and Jackson does not mean retreating from objectivity, but admitting that we never quite dump all of our personal and cultural biases, and realizing that objectivity itself can be a form of social distance in the study of other humans.

Any good-faith effort to engage another lifeway puts our own comfortable and familiar world at risk. The situation is somewhat
analogous to the words of the philosopher of science, Karl Popper, who
speaks not only of putting theories at risk with data, but actually seeking data that would falsify theory. Although anthropologists do not
enter the field specifically to falsify their own culture, they do put it at
risk (cultures after all do make statements about reality) because
another culture has another version of reality that contests our own.
Unlike theory formation, however, we are not likely to throw out our
own culture because it seems to fail the test of an alternative reality.
Being a reflexive fieldworker only approximates the act of putting theory at risk. More to Popper's point, however, anthropologists do place
their *theories* of culture at risk and seek data to falsify those theories.

INTRACULTURAL DIVERSITIES

Virtually all of us live today among myriad islands of human diversity within our own culture, but we too often fail to penetrate the
apparent differences that divide us from each other to find the bridge
that connects us. The enormous scale of contemporary life fragments us
into ever smaller units of shared experience. Social race and ethnic
groups, social classes, age and gender, and bureaucracy all supply bases
for social division. The implications of our discussion so far apply
equally to these home-grown diversities. The lessons are virtually the
same for intracultural dialogues as for cross-cultural dialogues. There
is the one caveat: when we live in our own culture we too easily convince
ourselves of how well we know it all. At least, when entering another
culture we generally realize that we have a few things to learn.

Anthropologists employing participant observation have examined a variety of North American diversities. Robert Edgerton (1967)
relied on extended first-hand contact as he and his associates examined
the daily lives of mentally retarded adults who tried to lead normal lives
outside the institution of treatment. Because a detailed description of
mentally retarded adults was lacking, their thoughts, actions, and emotions remained unknown in any systematic way. Edgerton found that a
key to understanding their de-institutionalized behavior lay in their
wish to pass as competent in everyday life, and thereby avoid the stigma
of being labelled retarded and incompetent.

Barbara Myerhoff (1978) studied elderly Jewish people, and Herve
Varenne (1977) detailed the structuring of diversity in a midwestern
town. Williams (1986) described a group of teenagers immersed in a
drug subculture. Newton (1993) and Read (1980) studied aspects of

homosexuality, and Robert Murphy (1990) probed the adaptive struggles of disabled persons as a result of his own declining health. Spindler ([1982] 1988) and Ogbu (1974), among others, provided in-depth studies of public schools. Weatherford (1985) studied the United States Congress. Moffatt's (1989) study of how diversities such as race and gender manifest themselves in college life at Rutgers rests on many days of participation and observation in dorm life over a decade. He documents as well the chasms separating students, faculty, and administrators.

Ferraro (1990) points out the value of studying domestic business organizations which contain "different social components that come from different backgrounds, hold contrasting values and attitudes, and have conflicting loyalties" (p. 6). He further observes that the awareness of "cultural environments" becomes even more important because of the erroneous belief that success at home guarantees success abroad. This ignorance is one of the most common causes of failure in international business.

ETHICS

Rapport rests on a respect for other ways of life, even outlandish and repugnant ways. Indeed, Stoller (1989:156) asserts that "a deep respect for other worlds and other ideas, ideas often preposterous to our way of thinking, is central to the ethnographic endeavor." Respect awards value to a people's imperfect struggle with life, a struggle which binds us all in common cause.

Respect for other ways entails certain ethical standards of behavior for outsiders, not the least of which is the protection of informant confidentiality and the reasonable security of collected data. Anthropologists work with informants, not informers. It is common these days to refer to those who "rat" or "squeal" on others engaged in illegal activity as informants. They are, in fact, informers, and have nothing to do with the work of social scientists. Informants, on the other hand, are those who instruct us in their accepted way of life, and deal largely with public life. Some research projects are, of course, more sensitive than others, and anthropologists certainly hear their share of gossip, accusation, and counteraccusation. However, data are kept confidential and every effort made to conceal identities of people, and even the site of the fieldwork. Anthropologists frequently face moral dilemmas and occasionally have lapses of ethical behavior but are normally exceedingly careful about how they conduct themselves in the field. Certainly they do not want to become known as insensitive, "ugly Americans."

The American Anthropological Association has, as do other organizations in anthropology, a code of ethics. Codes of ethics embody both a statement of philosophy as well as a code of conduct. The "Newsletter" of the American Anthropological Association has for years published a column on ethical dilemmas in order to maintain a high level of sensitivity to problems of ethics.

CONCLUSION

This chapter is intended to plunge the reader more deeply into the dynamics of culture contact. The best way to bridge chasms of diversity is to make the good faith effort to learn more about another way of life by investing significantly in first-hand experience with it. This precept is relevant to the needs of the diplomat, the development agent, the soldier, or the international business person, as well as the anthropologist. What constitutes a "good faith effort" or a "significant investment"? The phrases remain general because of the many conditions and contingencies under which people find themselves in first-hand contact. But they are meant to underscore the caveat that half-hearted, cookbook efforts are not only less productive, but likely to be more harmful than had an effort not been made in the first place.

The fieldworker should know that the questions he asks, the people he asks, and the contexts in which he asks them all bear importantly on his interaction with insiders. The fieldworker needs to be sensitive to the fact that asking and watching are not the same as participating. The fieldworker needs to know that the simple fact of visiting a people affects his or her relationship with them in ways that are often quite subtle, but important. The fieldworker needs to be careful in romanticizing relationships where there is apparently good rapport. The fieldworker needs to be aware of the explicit and implicit levels of ethnocentrism and to award others their basic humanity.

Chapter Six

Meeting the Challenge

Perceiving difference always bears the potential for prejudice and discrimination. Perceiving commonality bears the potential for inclusion and understanding. But it is sometimes hard to find our commonality when we seem so vastly different. We have emphasized the fact that groups begin to diverge as they encounter different circumstances and try to adapt to them. We have outlined a strategy by which to learn the reasons for the acts and beliefs that seem so unfathomable to us, while admitting that it is not foolproof. We ask how they have dealt with the world as given them, and award them, as we do ourselves, the imperfection of human effort.

We very often find ourselves poised indecisively on the question of emphasizing either similarities or differences, when we should see both as part of a single, unified model, our framework for understanding. The truth is that we are usually swayed in one direction or another by popular opinion which is generated in turn by the forces of history and competition rather than by an informed point of view. To recognize the influence of political or economic forces on our view of others, however, is not to succumb to their power. We can appreciate how these larger forces impinge on our lives, but we must counter their effect with information, concept, and perspective. It has been our task to provide you with these tools, the tools of discovery and understanding.

The act of comparing is an essential part of how our brain works. It is not simply that we observe that they do something one way and we do it another, but also the stance we take regarding the difference. What does the difference mean? What attitude or action should we take following our perception? To answer these questions, we advocate grounding our conclusions and inferences firmly in the real-life experience of others as they see it. In doing so, we need to be alert to the cultural sources of our reaction and sensitive to our forms of self-deception. Assessing and judging others inevitably accompanies comparison

99

and is usually based on our own unexamined patterns of thought, and that is why we are ethnocentric. We cannot discard comparison, but we can develop a more sophisticated and informed basis for comparison, and we can certainly jettison biased judgments based on hierarchy (better or worse) and simplistic views of morality (good or bad).

Cultural and subcultural differences are real, often serious, and frequently hard for the outsider to penetrate. Insiders sometimes react in anger and hostility to the arrogance of an outsider who has come to "understand" them. The chasm between the two may be so wide as seeming to preclude any chance that we can achieve some understanding.

Understanding has many levels of meaning. We cannot, of course, merge with the psyche, emotions, and memory traces of an individual, duplicate them in our own mind. We are all in that sense black boxes to each other even within our group. We are concerned here rather with understanding and predicting public behavior. We may, in fact, come to know individuals quite well, and they us, but we are more concerned with understanding normative action and shared motivations, norms, values, and beliefs. We are concerned with individuals' point of view and with grasping how they came to that point of view. These are certainly attainable goals for many people who are not anthropologists. We do not demean the science of anthropology by saying this, nor, on the other hand, do we wish to award the amateur a professional status. Professionals must answer to higher standards of evidence and more stringent arguments. There are many intellectual and emotional pitfalls awaiting us when we strive to sort out other ways, and even professionals fall into them now and again.

Engaging human diversity must mean engaging human commonality as well. We cannot otherwise untangle successfully the complex maze of diversity. It requires a discussion among groups in terms of their similarities and differences, and their self-examination. Dialogue requires a reasonable measure of mutual respect for each other's humanity.

These are fertile times for the politics of hatred and divisiveness. The culture wars we mentioned in the introduction are very much with us on national and global levels. Assertions and counterassertions about heritage and ethnic purity, about East versus West, and we and they, mark the day (Foster 1991). These contests—the politics of identity—involve varying degrees of ignorance or understanding of others, but they are mostly about differential power and wealth expressed symbolically—the idiom of cultural difference. Culture and ethnicity in this context become the bases for political protests and demands; they are the rationale, not the cause.

Culture conservation, which we encountered in our discussion of museums and primitive art, celebrates cultural difference by seeking to understand the "full range of resources people use to construct and sustain their cultures" (Hufford 1994:4). For those who have long suffered sustained and denigrating attacks on their cultural heritage, these efforts to award value and humanity to their way are generally welcomed, although not necessarily without reservation (Hufford 1994). Conservation permits both tradition and adaptation, permits cultures to change while preserving a valued past. This ideal does not seek to place tradition under glass to preserve it, much like a museum display, but gives it a living vitality.

Culture wars, culture conservation, and various issues of ethnicity and race, age and gender, and social stratification testify to our continuing struggle to answer the challenge of human diversity. We do not lack the tools by which to unravel much of the tangle, but whether or not we have the will is another question.

References

Agar, Michael. 1973. *Ripping and Running: A Formal Ethnography of Urban Heroin Addicts*. New York: Seminar Press.

___. 1980. *The Professional Stranger: An Informal Introduction to Ethnography*. New York: Academic Press.

Altorki, Soraya, and Camilia Fawzi El-Solh. 1984. *Arab Women in the Field: Studying Your Own Society*. Syracuse, NY: Syracuse University Press.

Alverson, Marianne. 1987. *Under African Sun*. Chicago: University of Chicago Press.

Anderson, Barbara Gallatin. 1990. *First Fieldwork: The Misadventures of an Anthropologist*. Prospect Heights, IL: Waveland Press.

Barrett, Richard A. 1984. *Culture and Conduct: An Excursion in Anthropology*. Belmont, CA: Wadsworth.

Barth, Fredrik. 1969. *Ethnic Groups and Boundaries: The Social Organization of Culture Difference*. Boston: Little, Brown.

Belmonte, Thomas. 1989. *The Broken Fountain*. 2d ed. New York: Columbia University Press.

Berry, John. 1976. *Human Ecology and Cognitive Style*. New York: Halsted.

Bishop, J. A., Cook, L. M., and Muggleton, J. 1978. The Response of Two Species of Moths to Industrialization in Northwest England: II. Relative Fitness of Moths and Population Size. *Philosophical Transactions, Royal Society of London*, 281:517–42.

Boas, Franz. [1940] 1966. *Race, Language, and Culture*. New York: Free Press.

Bodley, John. 1990. *Victims of Progress*. 3d ed. Mountain View, CA: Mayfield.

Bohannan, Laura (see Bowen, Elenore Smith).

Bourdieu, Pierre. 1984. *Distinction: A Social Critique of the Judgment of Taste*. Trans. Ricard Nice. Cambridge: Cambridge University Press.

Bowen, Elenore Smith (Laura Bohannan). [1954] 1964. *Return to Laughter*. New York: Harper & Row.

Brady, Ivan. 1991. Harmony and Argument: Bringing Forth the Artful Science. In *Anthropological Poetics*, edited by Ivan Brady. Savage, MD: Rowman & Littlefield.

Brown, Donald. 1991. *Human Universals*. New York: McGraw Hill.

Briggs, Jean. 1970. *Never in Anger: Portrait of an Eskimo Family*. Cambridge: Harvard University Press.

Burkey, Richard M. 1978. *Ethnic and Racial Groups: The Dynamics of Dominance*. Menlo Park, CA: Cummings.

103

Butler, Thomas. 1992. The Ends of History: Balkan Culture and Catastrophe. *Washington Post*. August 30, p. C3.

Campbell, Bernard G. 1987. *Humankind Emerging*. 5th ed. Glenview, IL: Scott, Foresman.

Carmichael, Stokely, and Charles Hamilton. 1967. *Black Power: The Politics of Liberation in America*. New York: Vintage.

Chagnon, Napoleon A. 1992. *Yanomamo*. 4th ed. New York: Harcourt, Brace, Jovanovich.

Clark, Kenneth. 1965. *Dark Ghetto: Dilemmas of Social Power*. New York: Harper.

Cole, Michael, John Gay, and D. W. Sharp. 1971. *The Cultural Context of Learning and Thinking*. New York: Basic Books.

Cole, Michael, and Barbara Means. 1981. *Comparative Studies of How People Think: An Introduction*. Cambridge: Harvard University Press.

Cornell, Stephen. 1988. *The Return of the Native*. New York: Oxford University Press.

Counts, David. 1990. Too Many Bananas, Not Enough Pineapples, and No Watermelon at All: Three Object Lessons in Living with Reciprocity. In *The Humbled Anthropologist*, edited by Philip R. DeVita, pp. 18–24. Belmont, CA: Wadsworth.

Darby, John. 1976. *Conflict in Northern Ireland: The Development of a Polarised Community*. Dublin: Gill & Macmillan.

Deloria, Vine. 1969. *Custer Died for Your Sins*. New York: Macmillan.

Despres, Leo, ed. 1975. *Ethnicity and Resource Competition*. The Hague: Mouton.

Devereux, George. 1980. *Basic Problems of Ethnopsychiatry*. Chicago: University of Chicago Press.

DeVita, Philip R., ed. 1990. *The Humbled Anthropologist: Tales from the Pacific*. Belmont, CA: Wadsworth.

DeVita, Philip R., and James D. Armstrong. 1993. *Distant Mirrors: America as a Foreign Culture*. Belmonte, CA: Wadsworth.

Draper, Patricia. 1975. !Kung Women: Contrasts in Sexual Egalitarianism in Foraging and Sedentary Contexts. In *Toward an Anthropology of Women*, edited by R. Reiter, pp. 77–109. New York: Monthly Review Press.

Dumont, Jean-Paul. [1978] 1992. *The Headman and I: Ambiguity and Ambivalence in the Fieldworking Experience*. Prospect Heights, IL: Waveland Press.

Edgerton, Robert. 1967. *The Cloak of Competence: Stigma in the Lives of the Mentally Retarded*. Berkeley: University of California Press.

Eller, Jack David. 1997. Anti-Anti-Multiculturalism. *American Anthropologist* 99:249–56.

Ekman, Paul, ed. 1982. *Emotion in the Human Face*. 2d ed. Cambridge: Cambridge University Press.

Erchak, Gerald M. 1992. *The Anthropology of Self and Behavior*. New Brunswick, NJ: Rutgers University Press.

Fagan, Brian. 1989. *Clash of Cultures*. New York: Freeman.

Feld, Steven. 1982. *Sound and Sentiment. Birds, Weeping, Poetics, and Song in Kaluli Expression*. Philadelphia: University of Pennsylvania Press. (2d ed., 1990).

Fernea, Elizabeth Warnock. [1976] 1988. *A Street in Marrakech: A Personal View of Women in Morocco*. Prospect Heights, IL: Waveland Press.

Ferraro, Gary. 1990. *The Cultural Dimension of International Business.* Englewood Cliffs, NJ: Prentice-Hall.

Foster, Robert J. 1991. Making National Cultures in the Global Ecumene. *Annual Review of Anthropology* 20:235–60.

Fox, Richard G. 1990. Nationalist Ideologies and the Production of National Cultures. *American Ethnological Society Monograph Series*, no. 2. Washington, D.C.

Freilich, Morris, ed. 1968. *Marginal Natives: Anthropologists at Work.* New York: Harper & Row.

Geertz, Clifford. 1973. *The Interpretation of Cultures.* New York: Basic Books.

Golde, Peggy, ed. 1970. *Women in the Field: Anthropological Experiences.* Chicago: Aldine.

Gordon, Robert. 1992. *The Myth of Africa: The Making of a Namibian Underclass.* Boulder, CO: Westview.

Gould, Stephen J. 1981. *The Mismeasure of Man.* New York: Norton.

Graburn, Nelson H. H., ed. 1976. *Ethnic and Tourist Arts: Cultural Expressions from the Fourth World.* Berkeley: University of California Press.

Hahn, Elizabeth. 1990. Raising a Few Eyebrows in Tonga. In *The Humbled Anthropologist*, edited by Philip DeVita, pp. 69–76. Belmont, CA: Wadsworth.

Hall, Edward. 1990. *Understanding Cultural Differences.* Yarmouth, ME: Intercultural Press.

Hammond, Dorothy, and Alta Jablow. [1970] 1992. *The Africa That Never Was.* Prospect Heights, IL: Waveland Press.

———. 1977. *The Myth of Africa.* New York: Library of Social Science.

Hannerz, Ulf. 1969. *Soulside.* New York: Columbia University Press.

Hanson, F. Allan. 1975. *Meaning in Culture.* London: Routledge & Kegan Paul.

Harner, Michael. 1968. The Sound of Rushing Water. *Natural History* 77(6): 28–33; 60–61.

Harris, Grace Gredys. 1978. *Casting Out Anger: Religion Among the Taita of Kenya.* Prospect Heights, IL: Waveland Press.

Hemming, John. [1978] 1987. *Red Gold: The Conquest of the Brazilian Indians.* New York: Macmillan.

Herskovits, Melville J. 1973. *Cultural Relativism: Perspectives in Cultural Pluralism.* New York: Random House (Vintage).

Hufford, Mary. 1994. *Conserving Culture: A New Discourse on Heritage.* Urbana: University of Illinois Press.

Hymes, Dell, ed. 1969. *Reinventing Anthropology.* New York: Random House.

Jackson, Michael. 1989. *Paths Toward a Clearing: Radical Empiricism and Ethnographic Inquiry.* Bloomington: Indiana University Press.

Kearney, Michael. 1995. The Local and the Global: The Anthropology of Globalization and Transnationalism. *Annual Review of Anthropology* 24:547–66.

Kluckhohn, Clyde. 1960. *Mirror for Man.* New York: Fawcett/McGraw Hill.

Konner, Melvin. 1982. *The Tangled Wing: Biological Constraints of the Human Spirit.* New York: Harper & Row.

Kottak, Conrad P. 1994. *Anthropology: The Exploration of Human Diversity.* 6th ed. New York: McGraw-Hill.

Leacock, Eleanor Burke. 1971. *The Culture of Poverty: A Critique*. New York: Simon & Schuster.

Lee, Dorothy. [1959] 1987. *Freedom and Culture*. Prospect Heights, IL: Waveland Press.

Levy, Robert I. 1973. *Tahitian: Mind and Experience in the Society Islands*. Chicago: University of Chicago Press.

Lewis, Oscar. 1959. *Five Families: Mexican Case Studies in the Culture of Poverty*. New York: Basic Books.

_____. 1961. *The Children of Sanchez: Autobiography of A Mexican Family*. New York: Random House.

_____. 1966. *La Vida: A Puerto Rican Family in the Culture of Poverty—San Juan and New York*. New York: Random House.

Liebow, Eliot. 1967. *Tally's Corner: A Study of Streetcorner Men*. Boston: Beacon.

Lutz, Catherine. 1988. *Unnatural Emotions: Everyday Sentiment on a Micronesian Atoll and the Challenge to Western Theory*. Chicago: University of Chicago Press.

Lutz, Catherine A., and Jane L. Collins. 1993. *Reading "National Geographic."* Chicago: University of Chicago Press.

Malinowski, Bronislaw. [1922] 1984. *Argonauts of the Western Pacific*. Prospect Heights, IL: Waveland Press.

_____. 1967. *A Diary in the Strict Sense of the Word*. New York: Harcourt, Brace & World.

Marcus, George, and Michael Fischer. 1986. *Anthropology as Cultural Critique: An Experimental Moment in the Human Sciences*. Chicago: University of Chicago Press.

Margolis, Maxine. 1984. *Mothers and Such: American Views of Women and How they Changed*. Berkeley: University of California Press.

Martin, Kay, and Barbara Voorhies. 1975. *Female of the Species*. New York: Columbia University Press.

Maybury-Lewis, David. [1965] 1988. *The Savage and the Innocent*. Boston: Beacon Press.

Middleton, DeWight R. 1981. The Organization of Ethnicity in Tampa. *Ethnic Groups* 3:281–306.

_____. 1989. Emotional Style: The Cultural Ordering of Emotions. *Ethos* 17:187–201.

Mitchell, William E. 1987. *The Bamboo Fire: Field Work with the New Guinea Wape*, 2d ed. Prospect Heights, IL: Waveland Press.

Moffatt, Michael. 1989. *Coming of Age in New Jersey*. New Brunswick: Rutgers University Press.

Molnar, Steve. 1983. *Human Variation: Races, Types, and Ethnic Groups*. 2d ed. Englewood Cliffs, NJ: Prentice-Hall.

Moore, Joan. 1976. *Mexican Americans*. Englewood Cliffs, NJ: Prentice-Hall.

Murphy, Robert. 1990. *The Body Silent*. New York: Norton.

Myerhoff, Barbara. 1978. *Number Our Days*. New York: Simon & Schuster.

Myerson, Julia. 1990. *Tambo: Life in an Andean Village*. Austin: University of Texas Press.

Newton, Esther. 1993. *Cherry Grove, Fire Island: Sixty Years in America's First Gay and Lesbian Community*. Boston: Beacon Press.

Nielsson, G. P. 1985. States and Nation-Groups: A Global Taxonomy. In *New Nationalisms of the Developed World*, edited by E. A. Tiryakian and R. Rogowski, pp. 27–56. Boston: Allen and Unwin.

Oboler, Regina Smith. 1986. For Better or Worse: Anthropologists and Husbands in the Field. In *Self, Sex, and Gender in Cross-Cultural Fieldwork*, edited by Tony Larry Whitehead and Mary Ellen Conaway. Urbana: University of Illinois Press.

Ogbu, John U. 1974. *The Next Generation: An Ethnography of Education in an Urban Neighborhood*. New York: Academic Press.

Penniman, T. K. [1935] 1965. *A Hundred Years of Anthropology*. London: Duckworth.

Price, Sally. 1989. *Primitive Art in Civilized Places*. Chicago: University of Chicago Press.

Rabinow, Paul. 1977. *Reflections on Fieldwork in Morocco*. Berkeley: University of California Press.

Read, Kenneth. 1980. *Open Voices: The Style of a Middle Class Homosexual Tavern*. Novato, CA: Chandler & Sharp.

Rosaldo, Renato. 1989. *Culture and Truth*. Boston: Beacon Press.

Rosenstiel, Annette. 1983. *Red and White: Indian Views of the White Man 1492–1982*. New York: Universe Books.

Sahlins, Marshall. 1985. *Islands of History*. Chicago: University of Chicago Press.

Sanday, Peggy. 1981. *Female Power and Male Dominance: On the Origins of Sexual Inequality*. Cambridge: Cambridge University Press.

Schieffelin, Edward L., and Robert Crittenden. 1991. *Like People You See in a Dream: First Contact in Six Papuan Societies*. Stanford: Stanford University Press.

Sennett, Richard, and Jonathan Cobb. 1973. *Hidden Injuries of Class*. New York: Vintage.

Serpell, R. 1971a. Discrimination Orientation by Zambian Children. *Journal of Comparative and Physiological Psychology* 75:312–316.

———. 1971b. Preference for Specific Orientation of Abstract Shapes Among Zambian Children. *Journal of Cross-Cultural Psychology* 2:225–239.

Siskind, Janet. 1973. *To Hunt in the Morning*. New York: Oxford University Press.

Smedley, Audrey. 1993. *Race in North America: Origin and Evolution of a Worldview*. Boulder, CO: Westview.

Spindler, George, ed. [1982] 1988. *Doing the Ethnography of Schooling: Educational Anthropology in Action*. Prospect Heights, IL: Waveland Press.

Spradley, James R. 1970. *You Owe Yourself a Drunk: An Ethnography of Urban Nomads*. Boston: Little, Brown.

Stack, Carol. 1974. All Our Kin: Strategies of Survival in a Black Community. New York: Harper & Row.

Stoller, Paul. 1989. *The Taste of Ethnographic Things: The Senses in Anthropology*. Philadelphia: University of Pennsylvania Press.

Tannen, Deborah. 1990. *You Just Don't Understand: Women and Men in Conversation*. New York: Ballantine.

Thomas, Elizabeth Marshall. 1956. *The Harmless People*. New York: Random House.

Thomsen, Moritz. 1969. *Living Poor: A Peace Corps Chronicle*. New York: Ballantine.

Turnbull, Colin. 1962. *The Forest People*. Garden City, NJ: Doubleday.

Tylor, E. B. 1871. *Primitive Culture*. London: J. Murray.

Valentine, Charles. 1968. *Culture and Poverty: Critique and Counterproposal*. Chicago: University of Chicago Press.

Van Gennep, A. 1908. *The Rites of Passage*. Trans. by Monika Vizedom and Gabrielle L. Chaffee, Introduction by Solon T. Kimbell. Chicago: University of Chicago Press.

Varenne, Herve. 1977. *Americans Together: Structured Diversity in a Midwestern Town*. New York: Teachers College Press.

Wallace, Anthony F. C. [1961] 1970. *Culture and Personality*. 2d ed. New York: Random House.

Ward, Martha C. 1989. *Nest in the Wind: Adventures in Anthropology on a Tropical Island*. Prospect Heights, IL: Waveland Press.

Weatherford, Jack. 1991. *Native Roots: How the Indians Enriched America*. New York: Crown.

_____. 1985. *Tribes on the Hill: The U.S. Congress-Rituals and Realities*. rev. ed. South Hadley, MA: Bergin and Garvey.

Whitten, Norman E., and Dorothea Whitten. 1988. *From Myth to Creation: Art from Amazonian Ecuador*. Urbana, IL: University of Illinois Press.

Williams, Thomas R. 1983. *Socialization*. Englewood Cliffs, NJ: Holt-Rinehart.

Williams, Nancy. 1976. Australian Aboriginal Art at Yirr Kala: The Introduction and Development of Marketing. In *Ethnic and Tourist Arts: Cultural Expressions from the Fourth World*, edited by Nelson Graburn, pp. 266–84. Berkeley: University of California Press.

Williams, Walter. 1986. *The Spirit and the Flesh: Sexual Diversity in American Indian Culture*. Boston: Beacon Press.

Zavella, Patricia. 1987. *Women's Work and Chicano Families*. Ithaca, NY: Cornell University Press.

Index

Adaptation. *See also* Poverty
cultural, 46–56
ethnicity and, 62–64
gender roles and, 60–62
to poverty, 48–56
relationships within systems
and, 60
Adaptational views, of arts, 76–77
Adaptive nature of culture, 37, 47
Africa, myth of, 77–79
African Americans. *See also* Africans; Black women
poverty of (1960s), 48–51
Africans, *National Geographic* coverage of, 73–74
Agar, Michael, 31, 86
Age, roles and, 18
Altorki, Soraya, 18, 93
Alverson, Hoyt, 41
Alverson, Marianne, 9–11, 16, 17,
20, 41, 78, 90–91
Amazon Basin peoples, 81
Anderson, Barbara, 8, 9, 11–12
Anger
culture and, 34
among Taita people, 41–42
Animals, cultural differences in
treatment of, 19–20
Anthropological linguistics, 4–5
Anthropology
cognitive, 31
divisions of, 4–5
fieldwork in, 83–86
strategy of, 3–5
Arab cultures

gender rules and, 18
role flexibility in, 93
Archaeology, 5
Art
of Australian Aborigines, 76–77
cultural judgments about, 74–77
tourist, 76
Australian Aborigines, art of, 76–77
Australopithecines, 24

Barth, Fredrik, 62–63, 64
Bathing, 10
Behavior
channeling of, 39–42
cross-cultural variation in, 36
cultural adaptation and, 47
culture as learned, 35–38
ghetto-specific, 50–51
human, 25–26
relationships and, 60
as response to poverty, 48–56
as system, 59
Belmonte, Thomas, 21, 51, 52, 53
Berry, John, 29
Bias, 100. *See also* Ethnocentrism
countering, 45
in fieldwork, 84–86, 89
Binet's intelligence test, 32
Biological anthropology, 4
Biological similarities, 24–26
Bishop, J. A., 46
Black women. *See also* African
Americans
National Geographic coverage of
indigenous peoples and, 73

Boas, Franz, 85
Bodley, John, 70, 71, 81
Body language, 13–14, 33
Boemus, John, 68
Bohannan, Laura. *See* Bowen, Elenore Smith
Botswana, 9–11
Bourdieu, Pierre, 74
Bowen, Elenore Smith, 7, 12, 18, 20–21, 30, 84, 92
Brady, Ivan, 85
Brain development, 24–25
Brazilian Indians, 69, 81
Briggs, Jean, 9, 18
Brown, Donald, 4
Bureau of American Ethnology, 83
Burkey, Richard M., 67
"Bushman Myth" (Gordon), 78
Bushmen. *See also* !Kung Bushmen; San people
Butler, Thomas, 63

Campbell, Bernard G., 25
Canning industry, in Santa Clara, California, 53–56
Carmichael, Stokely, 41
Chagnon, Napoleon, 9
Chicana women, and poverty in Santa Clara canning industry, 53–56
Child-rearing practices, 29
Children, English, 30–31
Clark, Kenneth, 67
Classification, racial, 26–28
Clinical analysis, 27
Clothing, 9–10
Cobb, Jonathan, 38
Cognition
   defined, 30
   perception and, 28–33
   tests of, 31
Cognitive anthropology, 31
Cole, Michael, 31, 32
Collins, Jane L., 72, 73
Colonialism
   fieldwork and, 84–85
   racism and, 66–68
Color, racism and, 66
Communication

complex, 24
cultural differences in, 11–14
food as, 15
signal (call) system of, 25
Comparisons, objectivity through, 65
Competition, vs. interdependence, 63
Complement, for roles, 40
Complex communication, as human quality, 24
Confessional ethnographies, 85
Conflict racism, 67
Consciousness, 40
Conservation approach, 101
   arts and, 77
Consumerism, colonialism and, 71–72
Context, social, 92–93
Control, through racism, 67
Cook, L. M., 46
Cornell, Stephen, 80
Cosmographers, 67–68
Counter-transference, 94
Counts, David, 16
Cro-Magnon, 25
Cross-cultural studies *See also* Intelligence tests
   of behavior, 36
   of emotions, 33–35
   perception, cognition, and, 29
Cubans, 56, 62
Cultural adaptation, 46–56
   by early humans, 47
   to poverty, 48–56
Cultural anthropology, 3–5
   as division of anthropology, 4
Cultural differences, 99–100
   in communicating, 11–14
   coping with, 8–21
   in gender rules, 17–19
   intracultural, 21–22
   moral dilemmas and, 19–21
   in sensory experiences, 9–11
   in social use of food, 14–16
Cultural homogeneity, 1
Cultural place, use of term, 10
Cultural relativism, 88

Cultural similarities, 23–24, 26–43, 99, 100
  social race and, 26–28
  thoughts, emotions, and, 28–38
Cultural transmission, 37
Culture
  as adaptation, 46–56
  emotions and, 33–35
  judgments about art by, 74–77
  as learned behavior, 35–38
  as meaning, 56–59
  participation in, 92
  sharing of, 37–38
  as system, 59–64
  tests and, 31
Culture and Poverty (Valentine), 84
Culture conservation, 101
Culture of poverty, 48–49, 50
Culture shock, 7–22, 86–88
  defined, 7–8
Custer Died for Your Sins (Deloria), 80
Customs, 8, 16
  exotic, 67–68
  socialization and, 37
Cycle of poverty, 49

Darby, John, 63
Dark Ghetto (Clark), 67
Data, quality of, 89
Deloria, Vine, Jr., 80
Des Cannibales (Montaigne), 69
Descent, gender and, 61
Devereux, George, 94
Differences
  nature of, 45
  perception of people by, 63
Discordance, 27
Discrimination. *See* Race and racism
Displacement, 25
Distance, social terms of, 30
Diversity
  challenge of, 1–2
  intracultural, 96–97
  multiculturalism compared
    with, 3
  understanding of, 2–3
Draper, Patricia, 60

Dumont, Jean-Paul, 17, 39–40, 92–93, 94

Early humans, cultural adaptation
  by, 47
Economic expansion, poverty and, 54
Ecuador, 12, 13
Edgerton, Robert, 96
Education
  colonialism and, 71–72
  Eurocentrism in, 3
Ekman, Paul, 33
Eller, Jack David, 3
Emotions, culture and, 33–35
Employment, poverty and, 54
Encyclopedists, 67–68
English children, 30–31. *See also*
  Child-rearing practices
Erchak, Gerald M., 40
Ethics
  code of, 98
  in fieldwork, 97–98
Ethnic Groups and Boundaries
  (Barth), 62–63
Ethnicity, 62–64
  intelligence testing and, 32
Ethnocentrism, 88
  explicit and implicit, 90
Ethnographic studies. *See also* Sensory experiences
  of cognition, 31
  of senses, 30
Ethnography
  bias and, 86
  "confessional," 85
  fieldwork and, 84
Eurocentrism, 3
Europeans
  colonialism, racism, and, 66–72
  judgments about art by, 74–77
Evolution, 24–26. *See also*
  Adaptation
Evolutionary psychology, 36
Exotic peoples, European contacts
  with, 69–72
Experience, culture and, 33
Explicit ethnocentrism, 90
Extensive racism, 26

External relationships, 60

Facial displays, 33. *See also* Body
    language; Communication
Fago, use of term, 34
Failure, poverty and, 50
Families. *See also* Poverty
    African-American poverty and,
        50, 51
Fardle of Fashion (Boemus), 68
Fawzi El-Sohl, Camilia, 18, 93
Feld, Steven, 30, 58
Fernea, Elizabeth, 15, 18, 19, 41
Fernea, Robert, 19, 41
Ferraro, Gary, 97
Fieldwork
    critiques of, 84
    culture shock and, 86–88
    dialogue of, 89–91
    ethics in, 97–98
    historical background to, 83–86
    intracultural diversities and,
        96–97
    and logic of discovery, 90
    objective distance, repositioning,
        and, 94–96
    observation, participation, and,
        91–96
    rapport and, 93–94
    response effects in, 92–93
Fischer, Michael, 85
Food, social use of, 14–16
Foster, Robert J., 100
Freilich, Morris, 18, 84

Geertz, Clifford, 38
Gender
    roles, 60–62
    rules, 17–19
Germany, ethnicity and competition
    in, 63
Ghetto. *See also* Poverty
    social deprivation theories and,
        67
Ghetto-specific behavior, 50–51
Goddard, H. H., 32
Gods Must Be Crazy, The (film), 78
Golde, Peggy, 84
Gordon, Robert, 78, 79

Gould, Stephen J., 31, 32, 36
Group living, culture and, 37–38
Groups. *See* Ethnicity

Habit, 40
Habitual behavior, 37
Hahn, Elizabeth, 13
Hall, Edward, 4
Hamilton, Charles, 41
Hammond, Dorothy, 77
Hannerz, Ulf, 49, 50–51
Hanson, F. Allan, 58
Harmless People, The (Thomas), 78
Harner, Michael, 91–92
Harris, Grace Gredys, 41
Health conditions, cultural differ-
    ences in, 20
Hemming, John, 69
Herskovits, Melville, 85, 88
High-status people, 13–14
Hispanic-Americans, 56
Hispanics, ethnicity and, 62
Homo erectus, 24–25
Hottentot peoples, 69
Hufford, Mary, 101
Human diversity. *See* Diversity
Hunter-gatherer groups, gender
    roles in, 61
Hunters, The (film), 78
Hymes, Dell, 85

Identity, social, 39–40
Identity politics, 3, 100
Ifaluk people, 34
Ilongot people, 35, 94–95
Images, and myths, 72–79
Immigrants. *See also* Mexican-
    Americans
    ethnicity and, 63
Implicational meaning, 58–59
Implicit ethnocentrism, 90
Incest taboo, 36
Indians. *See also* Indigenous people;
    Native Americans
    Brazilian, 69
Indigenous people. *See also* specific
    groups
    images of and myths about, 72–
        79

response to racism, 69–72
Initiation rites, 30
Instinct, and learned behavior, 36
Institutional behavior, 96
Intelligence, race and, 28
Intelligence tests, 31–32
Interdependence, vs. competition, 63
Internal organization of culture, 60
Intracultural diversities, 96–97. *See also* Cultural differences
Intracultural meaning, 59
Inuit (Eskimo) people, 9, 29
Ireland, conflict in, 63
Italy, poverty in urban areas, 51–53

Jablow, Alta, 77
Jackson, Michael, 92, 94
Jivaro people. *See* Shuar people
Jivoaroan-speaking peoples, 81. *See also* Shuar people
Jobs. *See* Employment; Poverty

Kaluli people, 30, 58
    implicational meaning and, 58–59
Kayapo people, 81
Keller, Helen, 38
Kinship, food and, 15
Kluckhohn, Clyde, 65
Konner, Melvin, 36
Kottak, Conrad P., 26
!Kung Bushmen, 60–61

Labels, 41
Labor. *See* Employment; Poverty
Language
    acquisition of, 24, 38
    communication differences and, 11–14
    emotions and, 34
Latin America, 14
Leacock, Eleanor Burke, 49
Learned behavior
    culture as, 35–38
    instinct and, 36
Learning, as human quality, 24
Lee, Dorothy, 56
Levy, Robert I., 33

Lewis, Oscar, 49, 53, 60
Liebow, Eliot, 49, 51
Linguistics. *See also* Communication; Language
    anthropological, 4–5
    sociolinguistics, 5
Logic of discovery, 90
Love, culture and, 34
Low-status people, 13–14
Lutz, Catherine A., 34, 72, 73

Malinowski, Bronislaw, 83, 84, 90
Maori people, 70
Marcus, George, 85
Marginal Natives (Freilich), 84
Margolis, Maxine, 61
Marrakech, 15
Martin, Kay, 61
Matrilocal residence patterns, 61
Maybury-Lewis, David, 14
Mbuti people, 19
Meaning
    culture and, 38, 56–59, 100
    implicational, 58–59
    intracultural, 59
    sensory experience and, 57–59
Means, Barbara, 31
Melanesian Islands, 73
Men. *See also* Gender
    in hunter-gatherer societies, 61
    patrilineal societies and, 61
Mercantilism, 66
Mexican-Americans, and poverty in Santa Clara canning industry, 53–56
Middleton, DeWight R., 35
Migrant laborers, 55
Minorities, 3
    fieldwork and, 85
    intelligence testing and, 32
Mirror metaphor, 65–66
Missionaries, 70, 71
    San people and, 79
Mitchell, William, 86–87
Moffatt, Michael, 39, 97
Molnar, Steve, 36
Montaigne, 69
Moore, Joan, 55–56
Morality, 41–42

race and, 28
Mores, 39
Morgan, Lewis Henry, 83
Morocco, 18, 89
Muggleton, J., 46
Multiculturalism, human diversity
    compared with, 3
Mundurucu people, 61
Murphy, Robert, 97
Myerhoff, Barbara, 96
Myerson, Julia, 92
Myths. *See also* Native Americans;
    Stereotypes
    about Africa, 77–79
    images and, 72–79
    about primitive artists, 74–75

Naive realism, culture and, 35
Nandi people, 17
Naples, Italy, poverty in urban
    areas, 21, 51–53
National Geographic, power of
    images and, 72–73
Native Americans, 70
    education of, 71
    intelligence testing and, 32
    resurgence and political action
        by, 80–81
Native peoples. *See* Indigenous peo-
    ple; specific groups
Neanderthals, 25
New Guinea, 16, 69–70, 86–88
Newton, Esther, 96
Nielsson, G. P., 1
Noble Savage concept, 68–69
    primitive art and, 75
Norms, 37
North American culture, reposition-
    ing and, 95
Northern Ireland, conflict in, 63

Oboler, Regina Smith, 17, 41
Odors, 9–11
Ogbu, John U., 97
Open systems, 60
Outsiders. *See also* Cultural differ-
    ences; Cultural similarities
    perception by, 28

Pacific region, 73
Pagan Cannibal concept, 75
Panare people, 17, 39–40, 92–93
Papua, New Guinea, 16. *See also*
    New Guinea
Participant observation, 96
Participation, observation and, 18,
    91–96
Paternalistic racism, 67
Patrilineal societies, 61
Patrilocal residence patterns, 61
Penniman, T. K., 68
Perception. *See also* Myths
    and cognition, 28–33
    defined, 28
    selective, 11
    tests of, 31
Plains Indians, 70
Pohnpei, 12, 13
Popper, Karl, 96
Poverty
    in African-American inner cities
        (1960s), 48–51
    as closed system, 60
    meaning of, 59
    in Santa Clara canning indus-
        try, 53–56
    traits of, 50
    in urban Italy, 51–53
    women and, 62
Powell, J. W., 83
Price, Sally, 74, 75, 77
Primitive art, cultural judgments
    and, 74–77
Progress, Western concept of, 71
Puerto Ricans, 56
Pure races, concept of, 27–28
Purist views, of arts, 76–77

Rabinow, Paul, 89
Race and racism
    classifications and, 26–28
    clinical analysis and, 27
    colonialism and, 66–68
    controlling people through, 67
    culture and, 26–28
    fieldwork and, 84–85
    human behavior and, 36
    indigenous responses to, 69–72

intelligence testing and, 32
Noble Savage concept and, 68–69
systematic racism, 66
Radical empiricism, fieldwork and, 94
Ranked societies, gender and, 61
Rapport
  ethics and, 97–98
  in fieldwork, 93–94
Read, Kenneth, 96–97
Reconstructed logic, 90
Reflexive behavior, 85, 88, 96
Relationships
  within culture systems, 60
  ethnicity and, 62–63
Religion, colonialism and, 70, 71–72
Repositioning, fieldwork and, 94–96
Residence rules, gender and, 61
Response effects, in fieldwork, 92–93
Return to Laughter (Bowen), 84
Rites of passages, 39
Rivers, W. H. R., 83
Roles, 40, 41, 59
  changes in, 62
  flexibility of, 93
  gender, 60–62
Rosaldo, Renato, 35, 94–95
Runa people, 77

Sahlins, Marshall, 74
Sanday, Peggy, 61
San people, 15, 78–79. *See also* !Kung Bushmen
Santa Clara, California, poverty in canning industry of, 53–56
Schieffelin, Edward L., 70
Schooling. *See also* Education
  intelligence testing and, 31–32
Segregation, of genders, 18
Selective perception, 11
Self, 40
Self-awareness, as human quality, 24
Sennett, Richard, 38
Sensory experiences, 9–11
  ethnographic studies of, 30
  meaning and, 57–59

Serpell, R., 30
Sex (gender). *See* Gender
Sharanahua people, 17
Shuar people, 81, 91, 92
Sight. *See* Sensory experiences
Signal communication system, 25
Siskind, Janet, 14–15, 17
Skin color, racism and, 66
Slavery, 71. *See also* Africa
  racism and, 66
Smedley, Audrey, 66
Social class, 38
Social context, 92–93
Social deprivation theories, 67
Social identity, 39–40
Socialization process, 36–37
  channeling behavior and, 39–42
  language acquisition and, 38
  and social identity, 39–40
Social race, 26–28
Social use of food, 14–16
Social welfare policies, poverty and, 51
Society. *See* Culture
Sociocultural complexity, gender roles and, 60–62
Sociolinguistics, 5
Songhay people, 30, 57
Soulside (Hannerz), 50
Sound. *See also* Sensory experiences
  as symbols, 58
South America, native peoples of, 81
Space, concepts of, 30
Spatial perception, 29
Speech behavior, 12–13. *See also* Communication
Spindler, George, 97
Spradley, James, 31
Stack, Carol, 51
Status, 40, 59
Status levels, touching and, 13–14
Stereotypes, 41. *See also* Race and racism
  of Africans, 77–78
  of Hispanic-Americans, 62
  poverty and, 55–56
Stoller, Paul, 11, 30, 57, 94, 97
Stratification, gender, 60–62

Street-corner activity, poverty and, 49–50
Style choice. *See* Italy
Subculture, 38
    poverty as, 49, 60
Suicide, 36
Sun Dance, 35
Survival instinct, 36
Symbols, culture and, 38
Systematic racism, 26, 66
Systems
    culture as, 59–64
    gender roles and, 60–62

Tahitian people, 33–34
Taita people, 41–42
Taste. *See* Sensory experiences
Taste of Ethnographic Things, The (Stoller), 57
Temne people, 29
Terman, Lewis, 32
Testing
    cross-cultural, 31–33
    of intelligence, 31–32
    of perception and cognition, 31
Theories of culture, 96
Thomas, Elizabeth Marshall, 78
Thomsen, Moritz, 12
Thought, perception, cognition, and, 28–33
Time, concepts of, 30
Tonga, 13
Tourist arts, 76
Traits
    of poverty, 50, 53
    racial, 27
Transference. *See* Counter-transference
Transition rituals, 39
Translation. *See also* Speech behavior
    emotions and, 34
Tswana people, 9–11, 20, 78, 91
Tupinamba people, 69, 70
Turnbull, Colin, 19, 29
Tylor, Edward B., 83

Unconscious behavior, 37
United States, gender roles in, 61–62

Urban settings, gender rules in, 17

Valentine, Charles, 48, 49, 84
Values, 39
    cultural differences and, 19–21
    hierarchies of, 41–42
Van Gennep, A., 39
Varenne, Herve, 96
Voorhies, Barbara, 61

Wages. *See* Employment; Poverty
Wallace, Anthony F. C., 37
Wape culture, 88. *See also* New Guinea
Ward, Martha, 12, 13–14
Weatherford, Jack, 70, 97
Welfare, poverty and, 51
Western art, 75–76
Western world. *See also* Europeans
    perception and cognition tests in, 31
    perceptions of native cultures by, 28–29
Whitten, Dorothea, 77
Whitten, Norman E., 77
Williams, Nancy, 76
Williams, Thomas R., 35
Williams, Walter, 96
Witchcraft, accusation of, 20–21
Women. *See also* Gender
    in Arab cultures, 93
    National Geographic images of, 73
    in patrilineal societies, 61
    in poverty, 62
    and poverty in Santa Clara canning industry, 53–56
Women in the Field (Golde), 84
World War II, gender roles and, 61–62
Wounded Knee, seizure of, 80

Yanomamo people, 9
Yerkes, R. M., 32
Yugoslavia, conflict in former, 63

Zambian children, 30–31
Zavella, Patricia, 53–54, 62
Zulu people, 70

DATE DUE

DEMCO